# ADVANCE
## THE BOOK OF ANDREW

*"The Book of Andrew* offers us an opportunity to participate in a miracle—a much needed miracle."—NED KELLY, M.D.

*"The Book of Andrew* must be published. This cannot be kept in a drawer or in the dark. It has to come out. So many people will be struck by this and experience a release and be healed by reading this book. I believe this is a book with a purpose, that it will lead the way for what is coming next in the Christian Church."—REV. DR. ERNIE DAVIS, RETIRED PRESBYTERIAN MINISTER

"At a certain point, grownups want their theology to match their experience. The Book of Andrew is simply and eloquently told, an eyewitness account of the man I always thought Jesus was: a gentle teacher whose message of universal love and acceptance for men and women, of any race, creed or sexual orientation, was so radical and threatening to hierarchies and establishments that it has not been accepted to this day.

"The message is simple: Everyone is a child of God. Following Jesus's teachings to their logical conclusion, there would be no need for religious wars, no need for anyone to commit suicide for being different or not good enough. Two thousand years later, are we ready to understand this lesson and carry it into our daily lives?"—DR. NANCY OFFENHAUSER, AUTHOR OF *HEALING CANCER PEACEFULLY: A MEMOIR*

"It is no accident that this inspiring story called *The Book of Andrew,* written thirty-five years ago, is emerging during this transformational time, when our culture is finally challenging its biased condemnation of same-sex love. This is a historic revelation, calling forth again the core message of Jesus, Andrew's Master and friend, that love is the healing balm for humanity, and 'Love one another' is the greatest commandment."—GABRIELLE BEARD, SOCIOLOGIST, PRESIDENT OF THE WOMEN AND WISDOM FOUNDATION AND AUTHOR OF THE FORTHCOMING MEMOIR, *NO WILDFLOWERS ON THE MOON*

"*The Book of Andrew* brings to light a deeper knowing of the healing ministry of Jesus to a world that is trembling in pain.

"This book holds within its delicate pages a power and strength and wisdom that can only come from God. When read with an open mind, its beauty and simple yet profound truths can touch and transform lives. As it proclaims with such eloquence, love in all of its manifestations is the only Source of our redemption.

"Honestly, I wept when I read it. It is something that needs to be read over and over and over again. Only then can its message be inscribed upon and lived through our own hearts."—REV. CYNTHIA A. FRADO, UNITARIAN UNIVERSALIST MINISTER, FORMER MANAGING DIRECTOR OF DEEPAK CHOPRA'S *GLOBAL NETWORK FOR SPIRITUAL SUCCESS*

"Reading fifty pages of *The Book of Andrew* last night stirred my soul and will do so to millions around the world, within our tribe and beyond. No wonder it's taken so long to publish. The world just wasn't ready, but it is now!"—GEORGE PIERSON, FOUNDER, CREATIVE MINDFLOW

"I keep reflecting on *The Book of Andrew*. It's beautiful and makes Christianity make sense in so many more ways, at last. I could never embrace so much of what's in the Bible. Realizing how much was changed in Jesus's teachings was a wonderful revelation."—CLAIRE LEWIS ARNOLD, CEO

"A masterpiece of a miracle!"—APRIL LOPEZ, STUDENT OF DR. BRIAN WEISS

"*The Book of Andrew* reveals a truly compelling and deeply compassionate teacher we have come to know as Jesus. While the intimate story of the relationship of Andrew and Phillip is significant, the teachings are fundamental to all spiritual traditions. It is a major source of inspiration, daily guidance and insight into our relationship with the Spirit."—LEROY E. ZEMKE, AUTHOR OF THOUGHTS FOR TRANSFORMATION, MINISTER OF THE TEMPLE OF THE LIVING GOD, ST. PETERSBURG, FLORIDA

"Written with the honesty and innocence of a child, but with the depth and simplicity of the world's greatest messengers. I could not put it down!"—MARK ANTHONY RIVERA, PHYSICIST

"The Book of Andrew dramatically evokes the time of Jesus and His disciples with the beautifully written and fascinating story of Andrew. In this recounting of a devoted disciple and his love for another disciple, author Charles Lehman and editor Bruce Gregory show much courage, beyond religious and gender controversies. Andrew's personal story is artfully interwoven with Jesus's universal teachings of Love and their remarkable synchronicity with those of A Course in Miracles. In today's increasingly awakening spiritual consciousness, Lehman and Gregory, in bringing Andrew to light, give us the supreme gift of spiritual truths applicable to our own lives."—NOELLE STERNE, AUTHOR, TRUST YOUR LIFE: FORGIVE YOURSELF AND GO AFTER YOUR DREAMS

"This book touched my heart. Its message is human, sensitive, and beautiful."—HEATHER FRIEDMAN RIVERA, RN, JD, PHD, FOUNDER, PAST LIFE RESEARCH (PLR) INSTITUTE, AUTHOR OF HEALING THE PRESENT FROM THE PAST: THE PERSONAL JOURNEY OF A PAST LIFE RESEARCHER, AND THE NOVEL QUIET WATER

"The Book of Andrew made me realize how beautifully human we all are. I am more spiritual as a result of this book. I was never a great reader of the Bible, because it did not seem real. This book brought this very significant time in history to life. Beautiful, bright, real life!"—MINDY ROSENDE, METAPHYSICAL BOOKSTORE STAFF

"Thanks for giving me an advance look at this wonderful manuscript. I think it will be inspiring, both to the gay community and to the spiritual community at large. I can see it becoming a modern-day spiritual classic, up there with A Course in Miracles."—FAYE LEVEY, TRAVEL WRITER

"'I tell you this day, Andrew, that you must be born again. You will live many lives, until you have learned all the lessons you must master. You will live both as man and woman. In some lives you will love only women; in other lives, only men, and in others both women and men. This is true for all mortals, even your brother, Simon....In truth, those we call mortals are immortal, from everlasting to everlasting. The body in which you dwell today is but the merest shadow of your eternal soul. Seeing that in different lives the same soul may love a man or a woman, what can it matter in the eyes of God whether you love a man or woman in this life, if only you love in God's name?'

"When he said this, my heart was filled with gladness that never left me thereafter, for I knew that it was right that I should love Philip."

*From Chapter Three*

# THE BOOK
## OF ANDREW

# THE BOOK OF ANDREW

## A PAST-LIFE MEMOIR

### Witness of a Gay Apostle

CHARLES CALE LEHMAN
BRUCE M. GREGORY, EDITOR

*with best wishes
from Bruce M. Gregory
October 5, 2015*

THE ROUND HOUSE PRESS
KENT, CONNECTICUT

Published by
The Round House Press
PO Box 744
Kent, Connecticut 06757
TheRoundHousePress.com
TheBookOfAndrew.com

ISBN 978-0-9823089-2-9
Ebook ISBN 978-0-9823089-4-3

Publisher's note: This First Edition was produced during the government
shutdown of 2013, when no Library of Congress numbers were issued.
The full Cataloging Data block for *The Book of Andrew* will be supplied
in the Second Edition.

The publisher wishes to thank Margaret-Mary Kelly and the Women and
Wisdom Foundation for their generous contributions to the production
of *The Book of Andrew*'s First Edition.

Interior design by Alison Rayner, London
Cover design by Beth Shaw, Stormcloud Studio, Munich

To God and everyone,
to God in everyone,
with love.

"A human being is a part of the whole, called by us 'Universe,' a part limited in time and space. He experiences himself, his thoughts and feelings as something separated from the rest—a kind of optical delusion of his consciousness. The striving to free oneself from this delusion is the one issue of true religion. Not to nourish the delusion but to try to overcome it is the way to reach the attainable measure of peace of mind."

Albert Einstein,
in a February 12, 1950 letter to Robert S. Marcus,
on the occasion of his son's death from polio

# CONTENTS

# Part Two

# INTRODUCTION

Divinely inspired spiritual teachings that help awaken and enlighten humanity did not cease to arrive 2000 years ago. *A Course in Miracles* and countless other received sacred texts, old and new, are evidence of that.

*The Book of Andrew* is today's restored gospel, the missing words of Jesus, including his blessing on same-sex love. Supported by credible witnesses, this past-life memoir came to a man named Charles Cale Lehman, starting in the late 1970s, through hypnotic regression and later nightly revelations. Though in the beginning he struggled with deep skepticism about the validity of these powerful memories, Charles soon became convinced of their worth and the need to write everything down.

Released after thirty-five years, this book's publication is also divinely timed. Though society has evolved somewhat in recent years, spiritual divisiveness and tragic childhood suicides caused by gay-bashing continue to sicken many Americans. *The Book of Andrew*, with its powerful statements from a newly discovered authentic Jesus, responds as nothing else can.

*Bruce Gregory—shepherd and editor of* The Book of Andrew, *coordinator of* The Andrew Project, *friend of Charles Lehman and key figure in the safeguarding and publication of this life-saving text—tells the book's story.*

" IN 1972, when Ken Wapnick, one of the earliest teachers of *A Course in Miracles*, first met Charles Lehman, he remembers being stunned to see 'a distinct vision of the name ANDREW written right across Charles's forehead.' Ken told his colleague, Bill Thetford, one of the two *Course* scribes, about his vision, who later shared it with Charles himself. As described in Charles's 'A Personal History' chapter in Part II of this book, Charles had been experiencing powerful psychic and mystical experiences, indicating that he had something important to remember in this life. He felt that not only did the 'something important' have to do with the normally distant issues of sexuality and spirituality, but that these issues were tied in with Jesus and his disciples.

"Supplied by Dr. Wapnick, the name 'Andrew' became the organizing key to unlocking the mystery. Andrew was the same name, incidentally, that a very young Charles had insisted his family should have named him.

"Charles's mystical and psychic experiences intensified after Dr. Wapnick's clue was shared with him until, in 1977, Charles felt the need to explore hypnosis in order to resolve the mystery. Bill Thetford, Charles's former lover and dear friend of many years, recommended that Charles see me for a past-life regression.

"Charles arrived soon after, an attractive, intelligent, solid individual in his fifties who happened to be gay, as I was. I explained the regression process, which involved staying conscious during deeper and deeper stages of relaxation and guided imagery. We started with a prayer. His first memory was of a deeply grieving medieval peasant farmer who had lost his beloved wife and was heartbroken. The power of this unexpected experience helped prepare Charles for what came next.

"Guided to another life, he saw himself as Andrew, alongside the Apostle Philip, both devastated at the distant sight of Jesus crucified, and clearly in love with each other. I guided him forward, and he described being with the remaining disciples after Jesus's final departure, all feeling deeply inadequate at now being responsible for carrying out Jesus's ministry.

"Charles found this experience powerful but very uncomfortable. He came back in a month to try again, but his skepticism got in the way. He left my house and soon after lifted a heartfelt prayer, 'If it is to be, let it be.'

"That night, and for a good number of nights to come, he was awakened at about four a.m. with a flood of images and words coming through, all concerning the lives of Jesus, Andrew, Philip, and the other apostles.

"The first week produced fifty pages of notes. By the end of 1980, most of the transmissions had been received, and by 1989 *The Book of Andrew* was complete.

"Before he died in 1999, Charles Lehman asked me to take over the book's publishing. I am so grateful to now be able to say, '*It is done.*'"

# PART ONE

## THE BOOK OF ANDREW

·I·

# A Childhood in Galilee

If you have ever heard of me, you know me as Andrew, so that is what I shall call myself. I was born in the town of Bethsaida, hard by the shore of Galilee, for my father was a fisherman, as was his father before him. I was the second of four sons, my brother Simon being seven years older than myself.

How lucky it was to be born at that time, in that place, and to have a father and a mother like mine! Aside from her smile and his laugh, my earliest memories were of our small home, the banks behind it spread with boats, oars, nets, and other fishing gear, and the sea itself.

The Sea of Galilee had many faces: On clear days the pale blue water danced with stars of sunlight. On calm nights, under a rising moon, a sheet of burnished silver and hammered gold stretched as far as the eye could see. Throughout the year, Galilee caught fire in sunsets and quenched itself in gray dawns.

At times a sudden storm would come, with great black clouds rolling end over end, shot through with lightning and tumbled by thunder. Then the branches of saplings on the shore cracked like whips, while the sea foamed and churned in waves as high as a man is tall. Whenever this would happen, my father and Simon rushed about, pulling the boats farther away from the waterline and bringing the other fishing gear inside the house.

When I was seven, a storm came up while my father and Simon were out fishing. My third brother, Thaddeus, was only four at that time; my youngest brother, Mark, was still nursing at our mother's breast. Every few moments after the storm began I would go to the door and open it a little, seeking some glimpse of my father and brother, but finding only blackness, the howling of the wind and the rain like sharp stones against my face.

Once when I opened the door a gust of wind caught it and almost pulled it out of its frame, dragging me along with it. My mother gave a cry and rushed to me. It took all our strength to close the door and bolt it. We were both wet through. Then my mother clutched me to her bosom and cried.

"Will Father and Simon come back safely?" I asked.

She smiled. "I am certain they will, for God is watching over them."

Even as she spoke, lightning turned the sky to white and purple fire, then crashing thunder split the heavens apart. Despite my mother's words of comfort and her smile, her eyes gave me a different message. I clung even closer to her and cried, "I am afraid!"

Thaddeus left the corner, where he had been playing with a toy boat made of braided reeds, and ran to us. He was too overcome with fear to speak; his face was red with tears. Mother held us both close to her bosom and said, "Be still, my children. Have faith that they will return. You shall see."

While the three of us were still clinging together there came a loud knocking at the door. I ran to lift the bolt. Father and Simon burst into the room, closing and bolting the door behind them.

Father looked first at Mother and then at me. He threw back

his head and laughed. "What manner of fish are these, Simon? Clearly they have just been hauled up from the sea, for look, their fins and gills are still dripping!"

Mother ran to Father and Simon, covering them both with kisses. "Oh, Jonah! God is good! How happy I am to see you! I feared you would both drown."

"Well we might have," Father said, "if it had not been for our son Simon, who has the bravery of an eagle and the strength of a young bull. As it was, we could scarcely pull the boat to shore, and I shall have to buy a new net."

Simon was as wet as the rest of us, but I could see that his chest swelled with pride to hear our father speak this way about him. Simon never forgot that he was the first born. I could not remember a time when he had been a child like me. He had always acted like a man who had no time for childish things and little patience with a younger brother.

"Come," said Father, "we are all together again, and safe. Let us dry our clothing and warm ourselves."

Except for storms like these, Galilee was a gentle, fertile land heavy with life. Fields of wheat and barley rippled in the breeze, shining leaves of olive groves caught the sunlight, and on the green hills flocks of sheep grazed, the shepherds tossing small stones to guide strays back within the fold.

From my earliest years, Father and Mother had taught me that there is but one God, a righteous, just and loving Lord, and that we Jews were His chosen people. When I first heard stories about the great flood which covered all the Earth, the exodus from Egypt and the years of exile in the wilderness, I could not understand how the angry God in these stories could be the same God Who watched over Galilee.

Bethsaida was not a great walled city like Jerusalem, but a town of merchants, farmers, shepherds, and fishermen. Still, caravans came from both the east and the west, bringing traders who bartered cloth, pots, and spices for grains, olives, wool, and salted fish. Only a few of our townsmen could read or write, but many could bargain in Latin, Greek, Phoenician, and Persian. From listening to the traders in Bethsaida, I myself came to understand many Latin and Greek words, though I could not speak either tongue.

While Bethsaida was a prosperous town in a fertile province, life was not perfect, for where on this Earth is perfection to be found? Our people had not been free since the time of Solomon. Through the tetrarch Herod, the Romans levied heavy taxes on the land. In Jerusalem itself even our religion had become a mockery. Our high priest served not God, but the Romans. If he should displease the procurator, he was replaced by yet another smiling hypocrite, of which there was an ample supply.

Among our own people, the natives of Judea looked down on those who lived in Galilee. They held us to be hardly better than pagans, as shrewd as Phoenician traders and lacking in respect for the Sabbath. Indeed, the land of Galilee had been settled by Jews only six generations before my birth. The very name "Galilee" meant "country of the gentiles."

What the Judeans disliked most about us was our unwillingness to surrender a tenth of all our olives, grain, wool, and fish to the false priests of Jerusalem, where the priesthood was one of the most common occupations.

If the Judeans held the natives of the shore towns of Bethsaida, Capernaum, and Tabgha in low esteem, they thought even less of those who lived in Nazareth, a poor town in the foothills of Galilee which lay to the west of the sea and off the main trade routes. Once I heard a Judean trader say that the babbling of a Nubian made more sense than Hebrew spoken by a Nazarene.

In our own town of Bethsaida, the merchants and growers of olives would have little to do with fishermen. To their way of thinking, all fishermen were a rough, boisterous lot, given to laughing, swearing, and drinking too much wine. On the market day when I first went up to Bethsaida with Father and Simon, I saw that every citizen who bargained with them turned his head a little to the side, as if we all had the smell of fish about us.

Even the hours kept by fishermen seemed strange and perhaps ungodly to our fellow townsmen, for often the best fishing was at night. Many times Father and Simon would check their tackle in the evening, fish through most of the night, market their catch in the early morning and sleep from mid-morning until early afternoon. When the moon was down they used to fasten torches dipped in pitch to the bow and stern of the boat, that they might have light.

Whatever the merchants and growers of olives might think, my father was not like most other fishermen. He was well liked by all the others, and sometimes in the early evening would share a cup of wine with our neighbors, for the sake of companionship, but his best friend was not another fisherman but a weaver named Saul.

Saul was a quiet, gentle man with large dark eyes and a smile more joyful than the laughter of most other men. Father stood a full head taller than Saul and could have carried him under one arm as easily as a man might pick up a small child. Nevertheless, Father had more respect for Saul than for the rabbi, the scribe, or any other citizen of Bethsaida. Indeed, Saul knew the Torah better than anyone in our little town and could explain its meaning in ways that made the word of God a living thing, rather than a set of scrolls in the synagogue.

During the first twenty years of their marriage, Saul and his wife Esther had no children, so that all those who knew them supposed that they would always remain childless. Yet, in the twenty-first year of their marriage – some two years after my own birth – Esther bore Saul a son, whom they named Philip. What a child this was! Even those who were not relatives agreed that he was the most beautiful baby ever seen, without blemish and never once crying after the day of his birth.

I was too young to remember Philip's birth, but years later my father and mother often recalled that Saul's and Esther's neighbors spoke of this as a miracle, holding that God had given them a son only because of their abiding faith.

As Saul was my father's best friend, so Philip became mine, closer to me than my own brothers were. We chased one another through the dusty streets of Bethsaida and learned the Torah side by side. So close were we that my father, Jonah, and my mother, Ruth, loved Philip as they loved their own sons, while Saul and Esther would often laugh and call me their first born or Philip's elder brother.

Within my own family, Mother and Father treated all four of us alike, yet both Simon and I knew that I was my father's favorite son, an unspoken truth that was a wall between my elder brother and myself. Perhaps Father felt a kinship of the spirit with me because I asked some of the same questions he had asked himself. Simon usually spoke only of the day's catch or the high cost of nets or where they ought to fish the following night.

Once I asked my father why those who had not sinned should have to atone on Yom Kippur. He stroked his beard with his left hand and smiled. Finally he said, "You ask thorny questions, Andrew. If I tell you that it the Law, that is not an answer that has any meat on it. The Scriptures tell us that the sins of the father are visited on the child, but if the Lord is just, how can that be? In truth I myself have often felt joyful inside on Yom Kippur and wondered why I should put on a long face. Let us ask Saul what he thinks, the next time we visit him."

One day, when I was eleven years old and Philip was nine, I went to his home and found him sitting in the doorway, with two great tears rolling down his cheeks.

"What is the matter?" I asked. "If anyone has hurt you, let him fight with me!"

Philip motioned to me to speak more softly, so that his father and mother could not overhear. "No one has hurt me. I am sad because our neighbor, the widow Rebecca, will die before the next Sabbath."

"Surely you are wrong. When I passed her home, she smiled and waved to me. Who has told you this?"

"No one has told me. I have seen it in a dream."

"Think no more of this silliness and stop crying, Philip. This dream is only a trick of the mind."

"No. Twice before I have dreamed things that later happened. Have I caused these things by dreaming them? Don't tell anyone about this, Andrew. They will say that I am possessed by devils."

The thought that anyone could suppose the most beautiful and best loved child in all Bethsaida to be possessed by devils would have made me laugh, but I could see how deeply Philip felt about this thing, and I would not hurt him for all the world. "Very well. You know that you can depend on me to keep your secret. Only stop crying."

I thought about this several times the next day, but soon put it out of my mind. Then, on the third day, I heard that Rebecca had died in her sleep and wondered about the meaning of Philip's strange gift that was so troubling to him. A number of times after that he told me of something that would happen, and it always came to pass, but neither of us ever spoke of this to anyone else.

Not long after this, my brother Simon was married to Martha, the daughter of a boat builder who lived near Capernaum. Martha was as cheerful as Simon was serious, a girl with red cheeks and twinkling eyes. She was like the older sister I had always wished for.

What a happy time this was! The gathering was so large that the house could barely hold everyone. Martha's father had bought wine for all the wedding guests, and the room was filled with the fragrance of incense. Everyone joined in laughing, singing, dancing, and clapping hands. Martha's younger sisters scattered pine nuts and roasted grain on the floor, that the married couple might have a happy life together and many healthy children.

The Queen of Sheba could not have been more beautiful than Martha in her wedding crown. Simon looked more joyful than I had ever seen him. The day before the wedding he had clapped me on the back so hard that he almost knocked me across the room, saying, "This is when a boy reaches his full manhood, Brother, when he marries!"

While Martha was talking with Father and Mother, she caught sight of Simon across the room, deep in conversation with her two uncles. She turned to my father and said, "Father Jonah, what a wonderful man is your son and my groom! See how his brows draw together in thought! I wonder what weighty matters they are discussing."

Father said, "You need not wonder, for I know. Simon is telling them what price fish will bring in tomorrow's market." Then we all laughed together.

The wedding party at Martha's home was followed by a party in our home, and afterwards by a party in the home of Martha's oldest uncle. When the wedding week was out and the last gift exchanged, my mother sat down and loosened her sandals. "I shall never be able to marry off all four of our sons, Jonah, for I will not have the strength."

"You have no cause for such worry, Ruth," my father said, "for our purse will be exhausted long before you are."

As night follows day, so grief follows joy. In my twelfth year a terrible illness swept through Galilee, striking mostly infants and men and women over forty years of age. Without warning, the strongest among us would suddenly be so overcome by weakness that they dropped in their tracks. Then they would take to their beds, wracked by fever and tormented by waking dreams that deprived them of their senses. Each day the breath came harder and harder, until it stopped forever.

Hardly a family in Bethsaida was left untouched, and it was through this cruel illness that Simon, Thaddeus, Mark, and I lost our beloved parents. Mother was the first to be taken from us. By that time Father was so stricken that he did not learn of her death for two days afterward. At first we thought that he had shaken off the illness, but hearing of his loving wife's death broke his spirit, so that once again the raging fever took hold of him.

Shortly before Father died, he came to himself and saw the four of us and Martha standing beside his bed. Though he could hardly speak for want of breath, he looked at his eldest son and said, "Simon, take care of your brothers."

"You know that I will, Father."

Then we heard a terrible rattle in Father's throat. His head sagged against his shoulder and his mouth fell open. All of us dropped to our knees beside his bed and wept.

## ·II·

# THE AWAKENING

Simon kept his promise to our father, but the first few years went very hard for us. After their marriage, Simon and Martha moved into a house near Capernaum, one which Martha's father had lent them until they could save enough to build a home of their own. Since this house was too small for the five of us, Simon and Martha moved back to our family home at Bethsaida after the death of our parents.

About a week after our father and mother had been taken from us, Simon said, "Andrew, I need your help. From this time on, you must put childish things behind you and become a man. You already know how to cast a net, and you are a good rower. You and I shall be partners in fishing."

In the beginning I was little help to Simon, though I did bring another pair of hands to our task. But as I grew in strength, so Simon grew in his skills, until all the fishermen along the shore would say, "If Simon can find no fish, there are no fish to be found."

Now that Simon and I spent so much time working, I did not see Philip as often as before, but we remained the closest of friends. About the time that I had become my brother's fishing partner, Saul resolved that Philip should learn to read and write, for it was a great sorrow to the weaver himself that he could not read the Torah, even though he knew most of it by heart. Therefore, Philip studied with the rabbi for more than two years, until his thirteenth birthday. Because of his love for his father, Philip worked hard at his studies. The rabbi said that he had never known a better student, nor one so devout.

Sometimes in mid-afternoon I would go to visit Philip and find him and his father seated on a low bench beside their home. Saul would ask Philip to write something in the dust. Afterwards, Saul would sit looking at the writing for a long time before asking, "What does this mean, my son?"

"This tells of the beginning of the world, when God said, 'Let there be light.'"

Saul could barely hold back his joy or his pride in his son. "Is this not a marvel, Andrew? I have known these words all my life, yet I cannot make them out. Truly, writing is a light to the understanding and learning the beginning of a new world!"

At times like these, it used to seem to me that the son was the father and the father the son, yet Philip remained very much a respectful child. He never boasted of his learning nor looked upon it as anything more than a gift of love to Saul.

I could not read or write my own name, yet Philip would defer to me in all things, not by my will, but through his choice. For reasons that I could not understand, it always gave him great pleasure to see my happiness or to do my bidding. Whenever he had some question in his mind, he would seek my counsel, as if I were some learned teacher or a man of great wisdom.

When I was in my sixteenth year, Simon persuaded two brothers, James and John, to become our partners in fishing. Until then the brothers had been working with their father, Zebedee, who had become too old and feeble for the life of a fisherman.

At the time they joined us, James was some nineteen years of age and John barely eighteen. But though they were close in age, the two brothers were as different from one another as Simon and I were.

James was a giant of a man and round as a barrel, with cheeks as red as apples. He was always laughing and jesting. He never forgot any story he had heard, and never ceased retelling it. He was the only man I knew who could humor Simon out of his darkest moods.

John was smaller than James, with the face of one of God's own angels. Like myself, he was something of a dreamer, but of a very different kind. Where I breathed in the beauty of the world around me, John was always asking himself questions about the things no man can see. He would wonder what it is that makes one man good and another evil, or seek to know what a devout Jew should do if he must break one commandment in order to keep another.

The two brothers loved each other dearly, and John would laugh more heartily at James's stories than anyone else did, as if he had never heard them before.

One day, shortly after the four of us had started working together, we were seining near the shore without our boat. As we were out of the sight of all other men, we had taken off our tunics, in order that we might later have dry clothing.

Seeing me naked, James said, "When you marry, Andrew, your bride will be a very happy woman – if she should live beyond her wedding night."

After saying this, he roared with laughter at seeing my face blood red, but John pitied me in my shame and drew his brother's attention from me by slapping the water with his palm, splashing James's face.

"So it is war!" cried James. "Then defend yourselves, for I can rout Andrew and you together."

Soon the spray was so thick about the three of us that we could hardly see, and Simon shouted, "Are you all children? Let us get back to work, for there is much to do. How can I keep a roof over my family's heads, when I am forced to work with simpletons?" His voice was edged with roughness, but I saw that he could hardly hold back a smile.

As the years passed, Philip and I grew into manhood, worshiping side by side and dancing together in time of festivals. How different we were from one another! I was the ox, while he was the antelope. My hair was the color of chestnut and tossed like straw in the wind. His was as black as a raven's wing and framed his face in curls. My skin was like leather from the sun, and my body hairy. He was nut-brown, with skin as smooth as the polished wood of the olive tree. I had the broad arms and square, rough hands of a fisherman. He was as slender as the willow, with craftsman's hands that gave voice to his thoughts before his mouth did.

Philip was the most joyous, most devout, and most beautiful youth in Bethsaida. Especially was he beloved of the very young and the very old, for he would never mock or taunt either, but ever treat them gently and with love, for in truth his own love for them was very great. Their joys were his joys, and their cares, his.

By the time I had reached my twentieth year, Simon had saved enough money to buy a piece of land on the shore near Capernaum, not far from the home of Martha's father. Within the year he began building a new home there. I had thought our old home in Bethsaida good enough for fishermen, but Simon's new house in Capernaum was to be three times as large. He said that Bethsaida was only a sleepy little village, while Capernaum was a thriving city.

Now that life was easier for us and our brother Thaddeus was old enough to help with the fishing, questions which had troubled me long before began to occupy my mind once more. There was much joy in my life, yet something seemed to be missing. I thought that if I had more learning I might be able to understand what this was, and wished that I could read and write.

Being well grounded in the Law, I knew in my mind all that it said, yet I could not understand it in my heart. To me it seemed that all beauty which came from God must be good, and that the worship of God should always be joyful, yet some points of the Law seemed to dispute this.

I knew that the Temple and the Ark were holy, but could not imagine these things made by hands to be holier than rocks or grass or trees or the beasts of the field, which were created by God. And if even swine were created by God, how could they be unclean?

The question that troubled me more than any other was this: How could God, being merciful and loving his chosen people, visit the sins of the father upon the son?

Because of these questions in my mind and heart about the Law, I decided to follow the teachings of John the Baptist, who told of the Messiah to come, who would lead us out of darkness into light.

Thus, through my wish, Philip and I became followers of John the Baptist. My brother Simon thought this venture on the part of

Philip and myself a waste of time better spent working, but would not interfere, since this was a religious matter. For Simon's part, he thought that we should follow the Law as it had been given to us by Moses and the prophets, rather than the crazed rantings of a grubby upstart preacher with soiled and tattered garments and matted hair.

By this time Simon was known as the most skillful and prosperous fisherman in all Galilee, with the most seaworthy boats. His greatest happiness lay in a fine catch or in sealing a bargain for good nets at a low price. When it came to bargaining, no man could best Simon, for there was a force within him which made others bend to his will.

Seeing how much our fortunes had changed since those early lean years, I hoped that Simon might take more joy from life, that he might see the beauty in God's creations, and that he might be kinder and more loving toward Martha and his family. Instead he more and more fell prey to violent moods. One moment he would be slapping me on the back and calling me "Brother" in his booming voice, and in the next he would be giving me black looks and playing the stern father.

In his darker moods he was sometimes given to strong drink. He seemed to believe that in it he could find some magic that would right his world. He would grow angry that I, having no taste for it, would not join him in drinking, and say that I behaved like some beardless boy. Twice he had forced wine down my throat, making me retch. Afterwards I knew that he was sorry for this but could not bring himself to tell me so, because this would not be meet for an elder brother.

Except for his drinking, Simon followed the Law strictly and provided well for his own family, our brothers and me, striking great fear and respect for the Law in all of us. But as he had shut joy out of his own life, he could not understand the simple pleasures that others might find in those things beyond the strivings of men, the things that may be shared by all who open their eyes, their ears and their hearts. Whenever I looked up from our nets to admire the beauty of sunlight on the waters or a clump of lilies near the shore, he would accuse me of wasting time and order me back to work.

One night, when Simon had gone out to drink with other fishermen, Martha and I sat up until the middle watch, wondering which of my brother's faces we would see when he returned. We both knew that it would do no good for me to go in search of him, since James was the only man who could persuade Simon to stop drinking when he had taken too much wine. For a long time neither Martha nor I spoke.

Finally she asked, "Do you know why he does this?"

"I believe so. All his life Simon has been looking for something that is missing in his life. He used to suppose that he could find it in a bigger boat, or in this fine new home, or in being the first fisherman in all Galilee. Yet now when he has these things within his grasp, he sees that it is not true. Because of this, he does not know where to look next."

Martha thought a while on what I had told her. "Yes, what you say makes sense."

I told no one that Martha and I had spoken of this, but a few days later Philip said to me, "Tell Martha that Simon will find what he is looking for, but not where he seeks it. In truth, he has no need to look for it, as it will come to him, changing his whole life for the better. Of this much I am certain, but I have seen nothing beyond what I have told you."

Of all the prophecies Philip had ever spoken, none gave me more joy than this one. When Martha had promised not to speak to anyone of the things I would make known to her, I told her of Philip's gift for seeing into the future, and word for word, what he had said about Simon.

As Martha listened, the concern which had lately dimmed her eye passed away, like a cloud scattered by a summer breeze. "Thank you, dear brother. With all my heart I believe this prophecy. It brings me more happiness and peace than I can tell."

One spring day, in late morning, Simon asked me to go to the village to buy some cordage for mending our nets. As I walked along the shore of Galilee, I was thinking of my elder brother and of all those things, happy and sad, which had befallen our family. Most of all, I was thinking about Philip's prophecy for Simon, what it might mean, how it would come to pass, and when.

As I passed a grove of small trees, I caught sight of a young man bathing himself in the Sea of Galilee, not far from shore. As I drew closer, I saw that it was Philip. Though he had been my best friend for many years, I felt that I was seeing him for the first time, and my heart was strangely stirred.

When he straightened up from rinsing his face and shoulders, the clear water ran down his body in little shining streams. He was standing almost hip-deep in water, a white cloth loosely wrapped about his loins, and the sun glistened in little stars on his wet skin.

At that moment by the shore, Philip was more beautiful than any woman I had ever seen, so perfect that I caught my breath. It was like awakening suddenly on a cold morning, in air more pure than any I had ever dreamed of. My heart beat faster within my chest, and I was stirred by a passion I had never known until then. I could not understand this new strangeness within myself, and wondered whether it was of Heaven or of Hell.

Over the years my friendship with Philip had ripened into a deep and joyful affection, but I did not know until that moment that I loved him as another man might love a woman. From that time on I understood what had been missing in my life.

Before this happened, I had supposed that one day I would marry like all other men, begetting sons and daughters. Now I saw that all my life I should love Philip, never a woman.

As Philip had been a part of the very marrow of my life from my earliest years, how could I not have known this before? And now that my eyes had been opened, what was I to do? I was so besieged by a mingling of wonder and horror, joy and shame that I could not put words to my thoughts.

When Philip looked up and saw me, he smiled broadly and waved to me. I waved back, letting him know through signs that I could not tarry. I longed to stay and talk with him a while, but doubted that he would smile or wave to me or ever speak to me again, if he but knew what I was feeling. In spite of this, I could not understand how anything so joyful could be called sin, nor why the Law should deny me the love that I now saw to be the very substance of my life, without which breath meant nothing.

Never had I felt so joyful and alive as now, nor so unclean. The burden of my sin weighed heavily on my heart, but I could not help dreaming how it would be if Philip and I should make love to one another. While he had followed me in all things, I thought that if he could read my mind and heart then, when we faced one another across the shore of Galilee, he would not follow me in this nor do my bidding, but would shrink from my touch as from a leper.

I hastened about my errand. When I passed again on my way home, Philip had gone. Still, the sight of him standing in the water remained before my eyes the whole day, and I knew that I should always remember how beautiful he had been that spring morning in Galilee.

Later that same day, after our evening meal, Simon asked me to go with him to our boats. While we were walking along the shore, he said, "You have two and twenty years now, Andrew. You should marry."

His words struck my heart like thunderbolts. I had hardly discovered that I loved before I was asked to renounce that love and to become something that I could never be.

"Let me stay and work with you awhile longer," I beseeched him, "for you still need my help."

"Surely there is no reason why we cannot go on fishing together," Simon answered, "but you must set up your own household now. You would have married years ago if Father had lived."

"But there is no woman whom I love."

"You talk like a fool and an idolater. It is not a matter of some silliness called love, but of duty and the Law. You know that I am the head of our family, Andrew. Since you were a stripling of twelve years, I have been a second father to you and to our brothers. You shall do as I say. Before the next Sabbath has passed, I will choose a wife for you and make arrangements for your betrothal."

*If you must betroth me*, I thought in bitter jest but also in earnest, *then betroth me to Philip*. But I understood that argument was useless, for I knew the Law as well as Simon did, and I could not stand against his will.

"So be it," I said.

All that night I lay awake, torn with love for Philip, wondering what I should do and what would become of me.

## ·III·

# THE COMING

The following day I heard that Jesus of Nazareth, a young rabbi and prophet, would be preaching in a nearby village. I resolved to hear him, for there was reason to believe that he might be the Messiah whose coming John the Baptist had foretold.

On any other day I would have gone straightway to Philip and asked him to come along with me, but I was so covered with shame that I dared not do so. If I had been forced to look upon his face, I would have blushed to the roots of my hair, so that he would know at once what I would not have him know.

I was downcast, for I had broken the Law. When I had looked upon Philip across the shore of Galilee, I had lusted after him in my very heart. Although I knew that I should always love him, beyond all reason and even without hope, I hoped that the teachings of Jesus might show me how I could atone for my sin and attain righteousness once more.

By the time I reached the village, Jesus had already finished preaching. As the crowd which had been gathered about him scattered, I saw a woman kneeling before him, kissing the hem of his garment. Jesus reached down, lifted her up and embraced her.

When she turned to go, I saw that tears were streaming down her cheeks and that her face was filled with joy and wonder. I could hardly believe my eyes, for I recognized her as an old woman of Capernaum whose back was so twisted that she could not take a single step without pain, yet now her back was straight and she walked as lightly as a girl.

While I was still standing there, like one struck dumb, Jesus turned and looked into my face. He motioned to me and said, "Come, Andrew of Bethsaida."

I marveled that he could know my name, but I understood as soon as I had looked upon his face that the world had never seen his like before, nor ever would again. Straightway I loved him, not in the earthly way that I loved Philip, but as a brother who had always been a part of my life.

His eyes were clearer and deeper than any I had ever seen. His steady gaze filled me with joy, peace, and wholeness, so that the storm within my bosom stilled. With a single glance Jesus made me understand that he knew everything about me, even those things which I myself could not know, and that he accepted me just as I was.

Then Jesus asked, "Do you love God, Andrew?"

"With all my heart, Rabbi."

"Then come with me, for you shall be my disciple."

Seeing that I had sinned against God in spite of my respect for His teachings, it seemed to me that I was unworthy ever to go to the synagogue again, perhaps even to live, much less to follow a man who was truly holy. Yet I would not speak directly of my shame, nor of the reasons for it. Therefore I said:

"I, Rabbi? Why should you choose me for a disciple? I am unworthy, for I have no learning. I cannot even write or read my name. I am only a fisherman."

"I shall make you a fisher of men."

Knowing that I could not hide my sin from Jesus, I bit my lip and bowed my head so that he could not look into my eyes. Finally I said, "But you know that I am different from other men, and unclean."

"Do you then have cloven hooves?" Jesus asked.

When he said this, my surprise was so great that I almost laughed, for I knew that he understood what I meant, and that this was weighting down my spirits, yet he treated it as a thing of no substance. I could not think how I should answer, or why a holy man should want a man like me as a disciple. I said only, "You know that I could never be a lover of women."

He smiled. "Yes, I know that. Neither are you a lover of men. In truth, you love only one man. Be of good cheer, Andrew, for Philip shall be one of us. You and Philip and I shall labor side by side in our Father's vineyard, for this is the joyous task that God has set for the three of us."

If I had been truly holy, I would have been overjoyed only by the prospect of serving such a remarkable Master. Instead, my selfish heart leapt within me at the thought that all my troubles had been swept away, as an autumn wind might drive the fallen leaves before it. Now I should not have to marry, and I would be able to share at least a part of my life with Philip.

Jesus spoke again: "All love is holy in the eyes of God, Andrew, whether it be the love of a man for a woman, a mother for her child, a man for another man, or a woman for another woman. You are as God created you."

Then I asked, "But what of the Scriptures, Master?"

"There are Laws of God and laws of man," Jesus answered.

"Men may write their own laws in God's name, though this is more blasphemous than any oath ever uttered. They do this that they might trick the unwitting into doing the will of tyrants out of fear and ignorance. Will you believe your understanding of the Scriptures, or will you believe me, who bring you a new covenant?"

"I will believe you gladly, Master," I said.

"I tell you this day, Andrew, that you must be born again. You will live many lives, until you have learned all the lessons you must master. You will live both as man and woman. In some lives you will love only women; in other lives, only men; and in still others, both women and men. This is true for all mortals, even your brother Simon. Yea, even my own messenger, John the Baptist, even he shall return to earth again, for though he fear God and do great works and speak words rimmed with fire, yet he loves not his fellow man but judges him.

"In truth, those we call mortals are immortal, from everlasting to everlasting. The body in which you dwell today is but the merest shadow of your eternal soul. Seeing that in different lives the same soul may love a man or a woman, what can it matter in the eyes of God whether you love a man or woman in this life, if only you love in God's name?"

When he said this, my heart was filled with gladness that never left me thereafter, for I knew that it was right that I should love Philip.

"You are a good man, Andrew. Though there will come a day when you shall doubt me and balk at following the path which I have shown you, yet you shall be more faithful to me and to my teachings than others who will win greater honor in the eyes of the world. Show me your hands."

I offered my hands to Jesus, palms upward. He clasped my wrists and said, "There is great power in hands, Andrew, even in hands that cannot write." When he touched me I felt as if I were no longer flesh and blood, but wholly Spirit and a part of all Heaven and Earth.

I asked, "Will you stay with us tonight in Capernaum, that I may tell my elder brother Simon that I will follow you?"

And Jesus answered, "Indeed I will, for your brother shall also be one of us, though not so gladly."

In return, I said nothing, but in my heart I doubted that this would come to pass.

## ·IV·

# THE FIRST SUPPER

When Jesus and I reached my brother's home in Capernaum, I did not tell Simon straight off that I would follow Jesus. If I had done so, my brother would have supposed that I was doing this only to defy him, in order that I might not have to marry. Instead, I told him only that Jesus was a great rabbi and prophet of Nazareth who would stay with us that night.

Being proud of his new home, Simon was glad to offer his hospitality. I could tell that he too had felt the power of Jesus and understood that this was one far greater than John the Baptist. I asked Simon whether I might go to Philip and invite him for supper also, in order that he might meet Jesus and hear him.

"Yes," Simon said, "and on your way, tell James and John to come along."

While Philip and I were walking side by side toward Capernaum, I told him about Jesus and the wondrous healing of the woman with the twisted back. I could not speak of the terrible burden of sin and shame which Jesus had lifted from me without revealing my love for Philip himself. I told him that I had resolved to follow Jesus, but I did not reveal that Jesus had said that he and my brother Simon would also be his disciples. These were the first secrets I had ever failed to share with him.

In spite of this, I was happier than I had ever been before, sharing Philip's company and knowing that I could love him without sin. From time to time I stole a sidelong glance at his face and saw that he was more beautiful than ever, in the full bloom of young manhood yet innocent as a child.

Once, before I knew what was happening, our eyes met. Philip gave me a look so deep, so full of both joy and pain, that my heart stopped. The deepening twilight around us seemed to glow, like clouds on a summer night kindled by unseen lightning. For the first time I dared to hope that Philip might love me as I loved him. I ached to speak words of love to him, to touch him, to hold him in my arms, to breathe in the scent of his body, to feel his lips against my own.

Within the space of a breath we turned our gaze from one another. Neither of us spoke for a moment. Then we both laughed and talked about the jests we had played on one another when we were children, keeping our eyes fixed on the road before us.

By the time we reached Simon's home in Capernaum, James and John had already come. Jesus and Simon were disputing the nature of the Law.

"Is it right that a man should break the Sabbath by turning his hand to work?" Jesus asked Simon.

"Indeed, it is not, Rabbi," replied Simon. "How can you ask this thing, when you know the answer as well as I?"

"What if you were going to the synagogue and came across a man lying beside the road, bleeding to death because he had been set upon by thieves? Suppose him to be stripped naked, so that you had no cloth but your own garment to bind up his wounds. Would you let him die?"

"You know I would not."

"Then it is well to remember that the Sabbath was made for man, not man for the Sabbath."

Simon said nothing further. This was the first time I had ever seen my brother bend to the will of another man, and without resentment.

After supper, Jesus spoke to all of us, to Simon, James, John, Philip and me, as well as to Martha, our younger brothers and Simon's children.

"I bring you glad tidings of a new covenant. This is a true saying, yet it is false. No one except yourself can bring you news of the covenant. You already hold in your heart all that it says. You knew it to the letter when you dwelled in the Lord's own house. I only call it to your thoughts once more. The unreal babble of the world so fills your ears and mind that you cannot hear the voice of God within your heart.

"Neither is the covenant I speak of new, though it is little like the covenant men speak of. God's Law is unchanging. It has endured and will endure, through all eternity. Even so, the words of God are newborn every moment. An ancient bough puts forth unfolding blossoms, revealing in themselves the sun's own light.

"Whence comes the voice of God? Neither from rocks of the mountaintop nor from a burning bush nor from the thunder. Its dwelling place is in the soul of man. Was not Moses a man, very like yourself? Am I not a man also, created by God and born of woman, even as you? The Law of God has not been given to one man or one nation but to each man and woman and to all nations. *You* are chosen.

"Although God's Law is as clear as sun on water, those who are blinded by this world can see it only as a far-off glimmer, fitfully hidden in mist. Thus would they take truth to be illusion, and illusion truth.

"The covenant cannot be satisfied by words alone. Though I shall speak of nothing but God's covenant throughout this life, I can disclose it to you only through parables and in those things I do. When it is only spoken by man's tongue, the Law means nothing. Lived through his being it is everything. For every act to which we lift our hand and every breath we draw is either of God or not of God.

"After a while we shall speak more of this. Indeed, we will make it our food and drink each day henceforth. For now I tell you only this: think on the one word 'love,' not earthly love that sets you apart and enslaves you, but love that makes us one in perfect freedom, the love of God, in all, of all, for all.

"I shall teach you so to love and so to live your life that men will mock you and persecute you. And the greater your love, the greater will be the rage of those with little understanding, seeing that you in turn will neither curse your persecutors nor disown your God. They will suppose you bolder than the lion, though what you have, in truth, is love, not courage. Where there is naught to fear, who should have need of courage?"

Something in each of us was touched by Jesus and his words. Tears were streaming down John's face. Philip looked as if he had learned the greatest lesson of all, one that would make his father very proud. Simon also had felt the power of these words, and I could see that he was deep in thought, struggling to untie the knots of meaning that had nothing to do with the price of fish. But neither John, James, Philip, nor Simon seemed to understand that Jesus spoke as if we were already his disciples.

I seized this chance to tell Simon that I would follow Jesus for a while and was grateful when he said that I was free to do so, speaking no further of my betrothal.

Then Philip asked, "May I follow you also, Rabbi? Together Andrew and I have followed the teachings of John the Baptist, and you are far greater than he." My heart beat faster at hearing Philip speak these words.

"Yes, you may," answered Jesus, "for now is come the time of my ministry, and I shall need more disciples than you two." As he said this, he looked straight into the eyes of Simon, James, and John.

Then Jesus told us a parable of a master going abroad who had given each of his servants fifty talents of gold in trust. The first servant had lent out the money given him, so that he had one hundred talents when his master returned. The second servant had buried his fifty talents and had given these back to his master on his return. Then the master beat the second servant and drove him away, giving his fifty talents to the servant who already had one hundred. And Jesus said that those who had increased their talents would be given still more, while those who had nothing would have even that nothing taken away.

The meaning of this story was too deep for me to understand. I could see furrows in the brows of Simon, James, and Philip, as if they too found it hard to fathom the parable. But John's eyes filled with wonder and he smiled, nodding his head as if this story answered some question which he had asked himself many times before.

Then James said, "This story of a master and his servants brings to my mind another story."

When we heard this, John and Philip and I looked at one another and raised our eyes to Heaven, for we knew which story James would tell.

"Once there was a wealthy man who lusted after his beautiful maidservant," said James. "While his wife and children were visiting relatives in a distant city, he sent the maidservant's husband on an errand to another town a half-day's journey away. Then he removed his outer garments and took to his bed, feigning illness.

"'Come to me!' he cried out to his maidservant, 'I have twisted my back and cannot move!'

"Now the maidservant was a good woman, faithful to her husband, but knew that which was in her master's heart, for she had seen him look at her in lust.

"When she had come to him, her master said, 'Bring warm oils and anoint my back with them, for this is all that will bring me to health again.'

"The maidservant heated oil as she had been told, but she also warmed wine, into which she had put a large measure of saltpeter. 'Drink this, master,' she said, 'for it will soon relieve the pain that troubles you.'"

Jesus laughed heartily at this, saying, "Indeed, that is a fine story which grows better with each hearing. This is a good thing, seeing that it has been told so often, since the beginning of time."

Then James laughed more than ever, striking his giant hand against his thigh. "In faith," he said, "you are no down-in-the-mouth prophet but a real man. I have a mind to follow you myself."

"I am glad to hear you speak thus, my brother," John said, "for I have also decided to follow Jesus, he being the holiest and wisest man that I have ever known, and a true prophet of the one God."

"What is this?" cried Simon to Jesus. "Have I not taken you into my home? Is this the way you would thank me for my hospitality, ferreting away my younger brother who is like a son to me, and my other fishing partners as well? Then what am I to do?"

"You also are to follow me, Simon," Jesus replied.

"On my life, no! Do not suppose because we are brothers that I am an empty-headed dreamer like Andrew. Would I desert my family and the trade of my father and grandfather to go about the countryside preaching and begging like one possessed by demons? Never! Have I not spent many years of backbreaking work to make myself the first fisherman in all Galilee, and to build this fine home?"

"If you are already the first fisherman in all Galilee," Jesus asked, "what more is there for you to do here? Come with me and I shall make you a fisher of men. Why should you waste your life bargaining for nets, when I will show you how to bargain for the souls of men and women, and none shall excel you in this? The best net ever made by hands will one day rot or tear, but the souls of men are everlasting."

While Jesus was speaking, I caught sight of Martha standing in the doorway. When she saw me look up at her, she smiled, for we both knew that Philip's prophecy for Simon had been fulfilled. Jesus had brought Simon what he had been seeking all his life. Simon protested yet awhile, but I knew from the look in his eye that he too had been caught within the net of Jesus.

When Jesus said that we should leave the shores of Galilee on the morrow, I hoped to forestall our going so that Philip might spend more time with his father and mother, and Simon, with Martha and his children. Therefore I asked, "Can we not go to Bethsaida for a while, so that you might preach to our old neighbors?"

"No," Jesus answered, "for the elders of Bethsaida have heard of me and fear that I may shake their authority by teaching the people to think for themselves. Even now the elders are plotting to turn the town against me. It would go better for you and Simon and John and James and Philip if we sow the seed of love and truth on more fertile ground."

"But surely the people of Bethsaida have a right to hear your message," I said.

"And so they shall," replied Jesus, "if not in Bethsaida, then elsewhere; if not in this lifetime, then another."

And so it came to pass that Philip and I, as well and James, John, and my brother Simon, became disciples of Jesus. Simon left his family in the care of our younger brothers, Thaddeus and Mark, who by this time had almost reached full manhood.

# ·V·

# PHILIP'S LEAVETAKING

When Philip and I parted that night, he asked me to come to his home the next morning, in order that we might be together when he told his father and mother that he would follow Jesus. Since he was their only son, we both knew that this would be a heavy burden for them.

On the way to Philip's house, I thought how saddened Philip had been when Jesus told us that we should not bring a change of clothing but only those garments which we wore. This troubled Philip, not because he was proud or vain, but because every one of the few robes he owned had been woven by his own father as a gift of love.

How fortunate I was to know Philip's family! Though my own father and mother were dead, Philip's mother, Esther, was a mother to me also, and I had two fathers, my brother Simon and Philip's father, Saul. Esther and Saul were the gentlest, most loving people I had ever known. They were poor in worldly goods, but their home was rich in love.

When I reached Philip's home, Saul and Esther greeted and embraced me, calling me their elder son. On this, which I knew would be our last morning together, Esther made a place at the table for me, as she had always done whenever I visited their home.

I could still see traces of Philip's beauty in his father's face, mostly in his soft, dark eyes, but the years of close work which had left their mark on Saul had given him a different kind of beauty, so that the corners of his eyes crinkled when he smiled. He had more hair in his beard than on his head, and this was now more gray than dark.

Esther looked far younger than her years. In truth, she had changed little since Philip and I were children. She was a small woman with a light step who sang to herself while carding flax or baking. Her bright eyes shone with the love of God, and with love for her husband, her son, and me as well.

After we had eaten, Philip said, "Andrew, tell my mother and father of Jesus and what he has told us, for your words are far more beautiful than mine."

"This is a man whose like the world has never seen," I said, "greater than John the Baptist or any of the prophets of old. He can look into the very hearts of men, and though he is the son of a lowly carpenter of Nazareth, he interprets the Law with more authority than the greatest scholar in Jerusalem.

"He speaks with the tongue of an angel and cleanses men of their sins with the living water of God's word, bringing light to those who dwell in darkness. He works cures that no man can and casts out devils. In truth, I cannot doubt that he has come into the world from God Himself, bringing a new covenant which shall not be for us Jews alone but for all men on the face of the Earth."

Then Saul said, "This is good news indeed! From what you say, Andrew, Jesus must be the holiest man who ever lived. Since you think so highly of him, are we to understand that you would follow him?"

"Indeed, I shall," I answered, "and I am not alone, for James and John, the sons of Zebedee, and even my own brother Simon, will follow him."

"Even your brother Simon!" Esther marveled. "This must be a holy man indeed! And where Andrew goes, can our own son Philip be far behind, seeing that he has followed your lead in all else?" She never left off smiling as she said this, yet her eyes grew moist, as Saul's did also.

"With your leave, Mother and Father, I too would follow Jesus," Philip said.

"Since we have never denied you anything within our power to give, would we deny you this?" Saul asked. "Though you are our only son, the light of our lives and the comfort of our age, can we keep you from God's work? When you have gone, there will be an empty place in our home and in our hearts as well. Yet it is a great honor for a poor weaver to know that his only son is a holy man."

As Saul said this, Philip's own eyes grew moist, and he rested his head against his father's bosom. Then Saul cupped Philip's face within his hands and lifted up his head, saying, "Since what you do is right and holy, my son, why should you be sad? This is a time for joy and celebration!"

"My heart is heavy," Philip said, "because I see that following Jesus will not be the same as following John the Baptist has been. This will not be a matter of a fortnight or a season, but of years. Therefore, I fear that we may never see one another again."

"Even if that be true," Saul said, "the memory of your presence will always be with us. Whenever I go up to the synagogue, I will see you worshiping beside me. In time of festival, first among all the dancers in my eyes will be you.

"Also, I know that wherever you may be, you will be safe and well, for Andrew will be with you. If you should take ill, he will nurse you to health again. If you should be in danger, he would defend you with his very life. In truth, we have not one fine son but two."

Then Saul turned to me and said, "Before you take your leave, Andrew, I must show you something."

He went to the table near his loom and brought back a robe, placing it in my hands. "What do you think of this?" he asked.

"It is the most beautiful robe that I have ever seen," I answered, "as white as a heron's wing and as soft to the touch as a spring breeze off the shore of Galilee."

"Truly, it is the finest I have ever woven. I did not know why I made it, since no one had ordered it, but a voice within me told me that I must, and that I would know what to do with it when the time came. Do you think that Jesus would accept it as a gift?"

"I have no doubt he will," I answered, "when I tell him it is given in love, and by the finest weaver in all Galilee."

Then Philip and I embraced Saul and Esther and took our leave.

Philip's sorrowful vision of the future came to pass, for neither of us ever saw them again.

# ·VI·

# PHILIP AND ANDREW

The things recounted here happened soon after Jesus had drawn all his disciples to him, while we were encamped near Cana. One day, when I knew that Jesus was alone, meditating under a tree at the edge of a small grove, I went to him. Though Jesus had brought me more peace and happiness than I had ever known, I had still suffered many sleepless nights for love of Philip.

"I do not know how to say that which I would say, Rabbi."

He smiled. "Then I shall say it for you, Andrew. You want to know whether you may tell Philip of your love for him."

I nodded, feeling the blood rush to my face and ears.

"If you do," Jesus said, "he will be very glad to hear it, for his own love for you is as strong. Long before your eyes were opened to your love for him, Philip knew that he loved you."

"If that is true, Lord, why has he not spoken of it?"

"Being devout, would Philip disobey those teachings which he believes to be the word of God? Can you not understand that he too suffers from the same doubts and fears that have so tormented you? A great battle rages within his bosom, yet he would rather have your friendship than risk your scorn. How can he know that you might not abandon him forever if he spoke of this?

"Though words of love for you have never passed his lips, surely you have read the message in his eyes. As he has followed your lead in all other things, so will he follow your lead in this.

"I tell you that your love for Philip and Philip's for you is holy, so long as you love in God's name."

My heart almost burst within me when he said this, knowing that I could serve my Master faithfully without having to renounce my love for Philip, for my very soul had been torn between these two.

When Jesus said these things, I went to find Philip, who was drawing water from a stream nearby. I walked slowly past my brother and the other followers of Jesus, though I longed to run as fast as my legs would carry me. I found Philip near the bottom of the slope, carrying two skins which he had filled with water. When he saw me, he looked up and smiled.

"Philip," I said, "I have a message for you."

"A message from Jesus?"

"No, a message from me."

Philip laughed. "A message from you? Since we have played together as children and shared every thought with one another, what could you tell me of yourself that I do not already know?"

"That I love you more than life and always shall."

Philip dropped the full skins as if they had been struck from his hands, spilling water all about the ground around him.

"And I you, Andrew. How I have yearned to hear you say those words! How I have feared to say those words to you!"

The two of us were so filled with joy that we were laughing and crying at the same time, embracing one another and dancing in circles. Yet in the next instant Philip's face darkened with sadness.

"But what would our Master say of this?"

"Beloved Philip, would I speak of this without his leave? He has said that our love for one another is holy, so long as we love in God's name."

"Then I am truly glad, for this is what I have felt in my own heart, in spite of the Law."

A few days later, when we were still encamped near Cana, Philip said to me, "Next to the privilege of serving our Master, having you love me with all your heart and soul is the greatest joy of my life. Yet I would have you love me with your body as well."

When Philip said this, my heart leapt within me at hearing him give voice to the thought I had not dared to express, knowing his devotion to the Law. And I marveled that for the first time in our lives, he had not waited for me, but had taken the lead.

"Do you think that Jesus would grant us even this?" Philip asked.

"I have no doubt of it, since he has said that all things are possible in love."

When finally we were able to speak to Jesus out of the hearing of our brothers, he was standing near a small tree, where he had picked up a fallen sparrow chick and returned it to its nest.

As we approached him, he turned to us and said, "I have been waiting for you and know what you seek. If you were born of the Spirit, you would not ask this thing of me. Yet you are men, and it is meet that you should show your love for one another with your bodies as well as with your hearts and minds. Therefore, love one another joyfully, knowing that your mutual love for the God Who created us all will forge stronger ties between you two than any bond of flesh.

"As God has given you to one another, you have no need of any man's blessing, yet I will bless you. Give me your hands." Then he placed my left hand in Philip's right and clasped both his own hands about ours.

"You, Andrew, and you, Philip, shall love and cherish one another so long as you live, and even in death you shall never be parted."

Philip knelt at the feet of Jesus and kissed the hem of his garment, saying, "Oh, Lord, you have brought us out of darkness and wretchedness into light and joy. What you have given us this day is greater than any gift man could bestow. You are truly the light of the world and God's own son."

"As you are also," Jesus said. Then he lifted Philip up and embraced him. "This day I shall send the two of you to Capernaum on an errand. When you have accomplished it, do not stop at your brother's home, but go to sleep in the grove beyond Capernaum."

Also, he said, "You should not speak of this to the others, most of all not to your brother Simon, for this thing is beyond their understanding."

That night, after we had reached the grove outside Capernaum, Philip and I lay down together beneath the trees, and for the first time I saw him in all his beauty, as God had created him. How splendid he was in his nakedness! His body was traced in moonlight but also glowed with its own inner radiance, so that I understood for the first time how close he was to God.

I kissed his lips, his hands, his eyes, his hair. The scent of his body was sweeter to me than jasmine. The sound of his voice quickened my very heartbeats. The touch of his skin made my fingertips ache with longing. Earth, trees, stars, moon melted away.

My beloved became my world, filling all my senses. Time itself stood still, so that I could not tell whether this was the briefest of moments or all I would ever know of eternity.

After we had made love, we lay side by side for a long while, touching without speaking. Then Philip said, "I have loved you longer than I can tell. How often I have wished that we might lie together like this, thinking I sinned even to dream of it. Yet tonight beggars all my dreams, and I know that our love for one another is not of our making alone."

As we lay together on that hillside near Capernaum, listening to the calls of the nightbirds, far from all other people, I felt that we were lifted out of ourselves, becoming one with all lovers who had been or would be, man or woman, young or old, Greek, Phoenician, Persian or Jew, lying together in heat or in cold, in hovels or palaces, or on another hillside in some distant land unknown to us.

After many hours we fell asleep, nestled together, thanking God for His mercy and knowing more peace and joy than in our whole lives before this.

## ·VII·

# A VISIT
# TO CAPERNAUM

After Jesus and the twelve left the encampment at Cana, we returned to Simon's house in Capernaum for a while, so that Jesus might preach to our neighbors and Simon might see to his affairs.

The first night back in Capernaum, none of us five from Bethsaida could sleep, for finding ourselves once more in our old surroundings showed us how deeply the man from Nazareth had changed our lives. After the others had retired we walked down to the shore of Galilee, past the hanging nets, and stood beside Simon's old boat.

For a long while none of us spoke. We listened to the lapping of the water against the banks. Farther down the shoreline, near Tabgha, we saw other fishermen's torches, doubled by rippling images of flame in the dark water. We heard the cries of the nightbirds, calling each to each. We breathed in the air of our homeland, the air scented like no other. These sights, these sounds, these aromas were a part of my earliest memories, bringing to mind my father, my mother, my childhood home, and those happy days Philip and I had spent together as children.

Since Philip had always been as close to me as my own heartbeats, I knew that he was stirred by the same feelings, and I supposed that John, James, and Simon were also recalling other nights along the shores of Galilee.

Simon ran his hand slowly along the bow of our old boat, as if caressing it. "Surely we have all taken leave of our senses. Why should four fishermen and the son of a weaver go about the countryside like wandering priests without a temple? Why not leave religious matters to the descendants of Aaron and return to our home and families and to those things we do best?"

"How can I go back to fishing now?" John asked. "Like you, I was born a fisherman. My brother James and I have passed many joyous hours on the Sea of Galilee, working and laughing together. But in my heart I know that I was always meant to serve God and Jesus. Somehow I knew this even before he came into our lives. If I should leave him now and return to fishing, then should I truly be like one cut off from his birthright, a stranger in a strange land."

Then James said, "I will not leave my brother. Besides, Jesus is the greatest storyteller in all of Israel. He could make the very stones laugh or weep. I have never known such good times or such companionship."

Simon was more than a brother to me. He was my teacher, my father, my childhood Law. I had never disputed him, but this time I could not hold silent. "We are not living in the age of Moses and Aaron, Brother. How can we leave religion to the priests, imposters thrust upon us by the Romans, serving Roman pleasure and Roman ends, imposters like the high priest in Jerusalem, coached in his holy-day duties like some Greek actor on a pagan stage? We have a priest who truly comes from God. As he has chosen us, then who are we to say we will not serve?"

Simon looked at each of us in turn, as if we were babbling in some foreign tongue which had no meaning for him. In all the years we had fished together, neither John nor James nor I had ever opposed Simon's will. He could hardly believe that all three of us would do so now. When he spoke again, his voice was rough with anger.

"How easy it must be for the three of you to talk this way! Among us five, I am the only one with a wife and family, though all of you are old enough to consider your duty to our people and the Law. You are men, but you act like beardless boys or fools who would fish with a net full of holes. Clearly it is no hardship for Andrew and Philip to follow Jesus, for they are as happy in each other's company as – as a lovesick youth and maiden."

Since I would never have been able to disown my love for Philip, I kept my peace, giving thanks that the new moon shed but little light. If Simon had seen my face then, he would have known that when he likened Philip and me to a pair of lovers, he spoke more truly than he supposed.

Simon continued, "Philip says nothing, but he is content to drift about from place to place, like a boat without oars, rudder or sail, forgetting his family duties. Since our return to Capernaum he gives no thought to visiting his aged mother and father, though they live nearby."

I had never before known Philip to show anger, but for all his gentleness, he rose to Simon's words like a colt stung by a bee. "You cannot know how much I love my mother and father, nor how much I miss them. If I choose not to visit them at this time, it is only because a second leave-taking, coming so soon, would go doubly hard for them, and for myself as well."

The five of us had become so lost in angry words that we still believed ourselves to be alone, until we heard the voice of Jesus behind us:

"Your spirit is troubled, Simon."

"Indeed it is, for standing here beside my boat, I know that I am still a fisherman and always shall be. I am neither a prophet nor a preacher nor a 'fisher of men,' as you would have it. My father was a fisherman, as was his father before him. Each man has his place in life and should do those things which he knows best. Would you not agree to this?"

"If we follow that line of argument," said Jesus, "then we would have to grant that I ought to be working wood, as indeed I have done, being the son of a carpenter. In truth, some of my relatives say that it would be far better if I were still working wood, rather than going about from village to village stirring up trouble."

Simon protested, "But you are a holy man and a prophet. You have been called by God, and you work miracles."

"You have also been called by God, and you shall yet work miracles in your time."

"But there is only one Jesus."

"Just as there is only one Simon, one John, one James, one Andrew, and one Philip. Each has his own place in the Kingdom of Heaven."

Then James spoke up: "Have you forgotten, Rabbi, that there are two of us Jameses?"

Jesus laughed, clasping James on the shoulder. "You are right, but indeed there is only one James of Bethsaida."

John and Philip and I joined in their laughter, but Simon could hardly check his anger. "How can the two of you waste time jesting when life is a serious business? No one knows better than I how hard life can be. As a young bridegroom barely able to earn enough bread for my bride and myself, I was saddled with the care of three younger brothers."

"And nobly have you fulfilled your duties to them all, Simon. If I sometimes make light of weighty matters, I do it not to mock you but to show you that there is a time for laughter as well as a time for work. Indeed, we work best when our work is joy."

"Can being an outcast bring a man joy?" Simon asked. "When we came back to Capernaum today, did I not see how strangely my old neighbors looked at me, holding me to be a man who had broken the Law, putting away his wife and turning his back on his family duties?"

"Now we have come to the core of the bitter fruit of discord," said Jesus, "for this is why your spirit is troubled. It is because of your concern for the opinions of men. But should you not be even more concerned for the opinions of God? Like you I am an outcast to my neighbors and kinsmen. I am not welcome in Nazareth, for I have abandoned the trade of my earthly father and I have never taken a wife. Still, I do our Heavenly Father's will that I may be welcome in His house.

"For the time being, I will put away all laughter. If you would talk of serious business, let us speak of the Roman yoke which oppresses God's people, and of how I have come to lift that yoke from their shoulders."

"Now you strike fire, for these are a man's words!" said Simon. "I would gladly follow you in such a venture, even to my last breath. But if you have come to raise an army, why have you not spoken of this before?"

"I raise no armies."

"Yet you could easily do so if you chose, for strong men of spirit would follow you as willingly as little children follow their father. Indeed, far greater numbers would rally to your side if you spoke more of an eye for an eye and a tooth for a tooth, and less of walking humbly and turning the other cheek."

Then Jesus said, "You are too much deceived by the appearances of the world created by men, where truth is not to be found. Can you not see that those who think themselves the rulers of the Earth are even more enslaved than those they subjugate? It is a far worse thing to work injustice than to suffer it.

"I come to free men's Spirits, not their bodies, by showing them the truth of God. He who has a free Spirit can never be enslaved, though he be shackled and cast into the darkest prison. On the other hand, he who has never learned the truth of God cannot be free in Spirit, even if all the world should call him 'Emperor.'"

"You talk in riddles," Simon complained. "I am certain that you know more than any other living man, but these seem to be mere words, with no sense in them. When a man is shackled, how can he be free? Is it because he has the will within himself to break his chains, rise up against his captors and slay them?"

"Not at all," Jesus replied, "for only that man who has learned the truth of God is free in Spirit, and he who knows the truth of God can never slay anyone, under any conditions. Rather, he conquers his enemies with love, making them one with himself."

"This talk is like quicksand," said Simon. "As soon as I feel my feet on solid ground I sink in more deeply than before. Can any Jew worthy of the name be one with a Roman? Is he not rather his sworn enemy? Can love break chains? Would it not make more sense to use a sharp chisel and a stout hammer?"

Jesus laughed. "Indeed, love can break chains, or even raise the dead. Stay with me only a little while longer and you shall see wonders you never dreamed of, so that you will come to doubt your own senses, but never my words."

"Very well," said Simon, "I shall do so yet a while, though I suspect you are like a shrewd wine merchant who says, 'Since you will not buy a skin of wine, try a single cup.'"

# ·VIII·

# THE MINISTRY AND TEACHINGS OF JESUS

How remarkable he was, is and shall be! Indeed, he came to us as God's own son. I, most of all men, had reason to know this, for I was unclean, but he cleansed me and made me whole, and purified me with the fire and living water of God's word. I had lost my very soul which he gave back to me. And though my love was sin in the eyes of all the peoples of this world, he would not change me, but took me as I was, making me see I was in truth a child of our Father in Heaven.

If he had chosen, he could have made the very ground tremble and roll with thunder at his every step. He could have shown himself in tongues of flame, so that all men would know him as the son of the King of Heaven and Earth and cry, "Lord! Lord!" and fall down and worship him.

Yet he chose not to do these things, for he was also man, reared by a lowly carpenter of Nazareth who was his earthly father. He came not to humble the kings and princes of this world but to serve the poor, the weak, the wretched and diseased, making them whole, raising them above all the powers of Earth and showing them the Kingdom of Heaven. By these tokens I understood that he was no false prophet or pagan sorcerer but the son of the one true God.

Can the son of God choose mercy and love over wrath and judgment? Jesus was more loving than any other man or woman on the face of the Earth, ministering to the sick, visiting the afflicted, feeding those who hungered and clothing the naked.

Can the son of God jest? Our Master jested often in his gentle way and in the words of a simple Nazarene. As a father loves the laughter of his children, so he enjoyed making us twelve laugh with an unexpected thought turned upside down, or a word twisted back upon itself, into new meanings.

"There are many," Jesus said, "who call themselves worshipers of the one true God but do not know that in truth they worship false idols. For the names of these gods are neither Baal nor Astarte, but vanity, ambition, worldly goods and power.

"There was a wealthy Sadducee who bathed himself and anointed his body with sweet-smelling oils and caused handmaidens to pare the nails of his hands and feet. He dressed himself in the finest raiment and put chains of purest gold about his neck and jeweled bracelets on his arms. On the Sabbath he went up to the temple, saying, 'Now I am truly fit to worship in the house of the Lord, for none shall bring greater glory to His name than I do.'"

We all laughed at this, for he called to mind men and women we ourselves had known, and in this way he showed us that the wealthy and powerful who would set themselves far above their poorer brothers and sisters, are but bags of wind.

"Why do I say to you that it is easier for a rope to pass through the eye of a needle than for a rich man to enter into the Kingdom of Heaven? This is because the riches of the Kingdom – the fruits of the earth, the fish of the sea and the fowls of the air – belong to no one and to everyone. These are meant for all God's children.

"There are enough of these riches for all, yet this is not the way of the world. Through their own trickery or the greed of their ancestors, a few have much more than they need while their brothers go naked and starve. Seeing that this is so, how can these few keep God's commandment to love their neighbors as themselves? I tell you that it is far better to go naked but to have a soul that is clothed in righteousness.

"To show that they have great virtue or special favor in the eyes of God, so that they rightfully own those baubles they clutch to themselves, the rich pay scholars with false learning and men who call themselves holy. They do this not so much to deceive others as to hide from themselves the knowledge of the emptiness which rankles within their own bosoms.

"All this they do in vain, since in their hearts they know that they do not own the one possession worth the having. Their souls are like worm-eaten wood, for they have broken the highest Law of all.

"In spite of this, I say to you that you should love the rich, who are your brothers and sisters. Though they would blind themselves, help them to open their eyes. Show them that the worldly goods they call most precious are like so many millstones hung about the soul unless their riches are shared with those who have nothing."

"Levi," Jesus asked, "where is this Kingdom of God that I speak of, and when will men see it?"

"Since you often call it 'the Kingdom of Heaven,' Rabbi, surely it is in the heavens, higher than any bird may fly, and even beyond the sun, moon and stars. We men cannot fly. Therefore, we shall see the Kingdom of God only when our souls have left our bodies."

"You are right in trying to see beyond this world," Jesus said, "for truly the Kingdom of God is more vast than the mind of man can imagine. At the same time, you err because you overlook the miracles at hand.

"The Kingdom of God is everywhere at all times. The very ground we stand on now is part and parcel of God's Kingdom, as are the deserts, mountains, lakes and seas. You will enter the Kingdom of Heaven as soon as you open your eyes, seeking not to turn the things which are God's to your own profit but sharing these with all your brothers and sisters."

"Thomas," Jesus asked, "how many senses has a man?"

"It is common knowledge that the number of senses is five, Rabbi, in that we can see, hear, taste, smell, and touch."

Then Jesus said, "I speak not of common but of uncommon knowledge. In truth, a man's senses are not five but twice five. As a man's visible body has an invisible soul, so does each of the worldly senses have its counterpart in Spirit.

"There are those who see, yet they are blind, as there are those who hear, yet they are deaf. By heeding too much the judgments of this world, they have robbed themselves of that second sight and second hearing which are God's gifts to everyone, even to those who are blind or deaf in the understanding of this world."

Then Jesus cupped a lily within his hand and said, "If you look upon this lily through the eyes of the world, you will see only a flower of a certain size and color. If you look upon it through the eyes of the Spirit, you will see it as a token of God's infinite goodness and love, and as a surety of life eternal.

"Even the most worldly would grant that a lily is beautiful, so this is an easy lesson to learn. But if you put the teachings of the world behind you, always seeing with the eyes of Spirit, you will understand that even the serpent and scorpion are beautiful, as are those unfortunate men and women whom the worldly cast from their sight, calling them loathsome.

"If you listen in the way of the world, you may hear a man cry out to you, 'Liar!' or 'Fool!' But if you listen with the Spirit, you will know this as the cry of one who dwells in darkness: 'Help me! I cannot hear God's voice nor see His face, wherefore I fear.'

"As God called out to men in ages past, would He be silent now, when His people live oppressed, under the yoke of the Romans? No. God speaks to men and women even today, giving aid and comfort to His children who love Him. Yet only those who listen with the ear of the Spirit shall hear His voice."

"Let us proclaim the one God, the God of His chosen people the Jews, Who is also the God of His chosen people the Egyptians, Greeks, Phoenicians, and Romans.

"If a child should be born of a Persian and a Canaanite, of what tribe is that child? Do not the people of all tribes have two eyes, two ears, and ten fingers? Do not all shiver in the blasts of winter and sweat under the summer sun?

"If you suppose that there are many tribes, it is only because you see others with worldly eyes and hear them with worldly ears. You make much of differences in their speech, the color of their skins, or the set of their cheekbones, but the many tribes you see are creatures of illusion, phantoms of your mind.

"In truth, as there is only one God, so there is only one tribe. As we are all sons of Adam and daughters of Eve, we are all brothers and sisters. Who, then, is your enemy?

"And if we are all of one tribe, so we have but one God, though men call Him by different names and worship Him in diverse ways, according to their understanding. Let all the people of the Earth raise songs of thanksgiving to the one God Who dwells in all our hearts.

"If we grant that we own nothing, save our love for God and our neighbor, then we have all. Love is the one eternal treasure, the treasure no enemy can seize, the fortress that is proof against all attack, the one jewel beyond price that no man may take from us, for we give it freely to all."

Jesus turned to the one disciple whom I could not love, and asked, "Judas, what is sin?"

"That is an easy question to answer, Master, for if a man should take the name of the Lord in vain, or worship graven images, or steal, or kill, or break any of the other commandments, then he has sinned."

"You are right in supposing that the question is easy to answer," Jesus said, "yet you have answered it wrongly, for sin lies not so much in those things which we do, as in what we fail to do. Remember that I have given you two commandments which stand above all others: That you should love God with all your heart and with all your soul and with all your mind, and that you should love your neighbor as yourself. Anyone who keeps these two commandments cannot sin. Blessed is that man who loses in love all thoughts for the salvation of his own soul, for only such a man shall find salvation.

"If your father and mother should say to you, 'Slay your enemies! Wreak vengeance on those who do evil to you, taking an eye for an eye and a tooth for a tooth,' then I say, 'Dishonor your father and mother, for you have no enemies, only brothers and sisters.'

"The Law which was first given to God's chosen was well suited for the people of that time, who were simple, with little guile and no arts of interpretation. In the many generations since then, men as wily as foxes have sprung up, disputing God's Law as they would argue man-made laws in worldly courts, seeking how they might safely keep the letter of His commandments yet violate their Spirit.

"Therefore, I have given you two commandments which lie beyond all worldly dispute, being of the Spirit and only of the Spirit. Though future generations of false worshipers will seek to bury these commandments in trifling regulations and ritual that has no meaning, this new covenant shall stand like a rock against all assaults."

As we sat in a circle on the ground, Jesus said to us, "Attend me closely, for some will find this a hard lesson, although nothing could be simpler.

"Surely you understand that you are to love God with all your heart and with all your soul. Many will suppose that is enough. Yet I have also told you that you should love God with all your mind. What do I mean by that?

"The purpose of the mind is always to search for the truth beyond appearances, with each using his mind according to the gifts that God has given him. The mind thinks on what the eyes have seen and what the ears have heard. Also, the mind tells the hands what they should do. The journey of the mind is never finished. Ever there is truth beyond truth, for you cannot know the whole truth so long as you are trapped in the illusions of this world.

"The madness of the world is such that those in authority may be men of little understanding, whether they be called priest, procurator, or emperor. Love them, as you must love all people, but do not take for truth every word that passes their lips.

"Some hold that, because an ancient prophet has inscribed words on a scroll, those words must need be true. Yet I tell you that even those writings called sacred, being set down by men, mix truth with error. Do not learn these words by rote, but turn them over in your mind, according to the understanding God has given you, asking yourself whether these writings are truly of the Spirit, or whether they serve the worldly ends of those who seek dominion over others.

"Those who have received the gift of healing must use their minds, as well as their hands and Spirit. Unbelievers may not be cured by the laying on of hands, but some of these can be helped in other ways. This is why God has given some men and women knowledge of herbs and the gift of devising medicines.

"Heart and soul and mind must each receive its just and equal due. Those who prize the gifts of the mind above all else fall into serious error, for they may suppose that they have seen the face of Heaven itself, finding there no god beyond themselves. Yet even these, so long as they earnestly seek the truth, serve the ends of God, without their knowledge. In time all errors will be corrected."

One day the other James asked Jesus, "Rabbi, how should we pray?"

And Jesus answered, "I have given you the only prayer you shall ever need, but you are also free to create your own prayers, and to make of your life a prayer without words, by serving God with your whole being. You may begin by praying thus:

"Our Father in Heaven, I love You, I praise You, I give thanks to You for the blessing of eternal life. Show me that sin is illusion, that only Your joy is real, seeing that I am forgiven as I forgive. Lead me not into temptation but deliver me from my own hardness of heart.

"Let all my brothers and sisters share the daily bread which You have given. Help me to love all of Your other children as I love myself, that together we may enter Your Kingdom, for this is Your will. Amen.

"You have no need to pray for other worldly things. Should you pray for land or riches, when that which is given to you is taken from your brothers? Should you pray that this earthly life might be prolonged, knowing that your soul can never die?

"Should you pray for victory in battle over so-called enemies, seeing that this would mean death or defeat for your kinsmen? Should you pray that worldly leaders might be strengthened, that they might lead you into greater error?

"No, do not pray for any of these, for when you do, you sit in judgment, doubting God's mercy and denying His will."

"Labbaeus, what is meant by the saying, 'Even a child is known by his own doings, whether these be good or evil'?"

"Surely this is a true saying known to all of us, yet I find it difficult to interpret, for the words carry their own meaning."

"Do not believe it," Jesus said. "Men use words to hide meaning, not to uncover it. If the meaning is clear, tell me this: Who is the child the saying speaks of?"

"Surely a child is a boy who has not reached manhood, or a girl who is not yet a woman."

"In the eyes of God," Jesus said, "we are all children, even grey-bearded men and women stooped with age. But tell me further: Who is to know if the child's doings be good or evil'?"

"Why, everyone would know, since all of us know right from wrong."

"You are thinking in the way of the world and not in the way of the Spirit. Have I not said to you, 'Judge not that you be not judged'? But tell me this: If you see that the child's doings are indeed evil, what should you do?"

"I should point out his error and show him the right thing to do."

"That in itself would be an error," said Jesus, "for all you should do is love him all the more. The child who knows perfect love can do no wrong. It is only the want of love that leads children into error."

Then Labbaeus scratched his head and asked, "But if a child does wrong and goes on to do more wrong, who will correct the error?"

"God will correct it in time," Jesus answered, "through the love we show which comes from God. Our love is all that can open the ears of others to the voice of the Holy Spirit within their own bosoms.

"This is the hardest lesson of love. It is far easier for a Jew to love a Roman or a Greek who thinks like himself than to love another Jew who thinks differently. Such a Jew will say to himself, 'How can it be that he and I were both given the covenant, yet I think rightly and he thinks wrongly? How can it be that I do those things which we ought to do, but he does those things which we ought not to do?'

"When I say to you that sin is illusion, I do not mean your own sins only."

One day Jesus looked straight into my own eyes, fixing his gaze so strongly upon me that I could see only his face. "You say that you love God, Andrew. Why do you love Him? Is it because the Scriptures tell us that we must?"

"I have always tried to obey the Law," I answered, "but I love God still more because He has given us the world, spread before us in colors all the dye makers of Tyre cannot equal. Wherever we turn, God's world delights our eyes: in the olive tree heavy with fruit, in the newborn lamb on faltering legs following its mother, in groves of cedars swaying before the gathering storm. Moreover, God has given us a never-ending feast for all our other senses as well: the call of the turtle dove, the scent of damp earth after rain, the sharp sweetness of grapes upon the tongue. Surely all these things testify to the glory and majesty of the Lord."

Then Jesus said, "You speak of a world which you yourself have created."

"How can it be that I have created the world, when travelers tell of lands I do not know and wonders I have never seen?"

"If you should journey to these foreign lands," Jesus replied, "you would make of them what they are not, for your eyes have never pierced the veil of illusion. You are blind to the true nature of God's creation. You have come further along than those who would possess this earthly kingdom, that they might keep its riches from their brothers, but if you love God only for those things which are the creatures of your own earthly senses, you must find another reason."

"What is this other reason?"

"If I should tell you, my answer would be mere words to you. The true answer to the question you have asked lies beyond words and even beyond the earthly senses."

"If you will not tell me and if I cannot see or hear or touch the answer, then where am I to find it?"

"Search your own heart and call upon the Lord."

"Who do men say I am?" Jesus asked my elder brother.

"Some say Elijah. Some say John the Baptist."

"But who do you say that I am?"

"I say that you are God's only son and the Messiah."

"Am I God's only son? Have I not told you that all the peoples of the Earth are children of God?"

"But there is none like you."

"Then how have I become the only son of God?"

"It is because He has chosen you."

"That is true, but God has chosen everyone. If I am unlike other men, it is not that God has chosen me, but that I have chosen God. Having learned all the lessons of Heaven, I choose to do our Father's will rather than my own. In this way I have gained perfect freedom over the madness and death of the world of men.

"Men say that I work miracles. These miracles are but the power of God made visible through me. He is the Master, I am but the tool.

"Through love and the power of God I have given sight to those whom the world calls blind. This is as nothing. It is a much harder thing to heal the blindness of those who see and believe the illusions of the world of men but not the truth of the Spirit, for understanding comes only from within. The eyes of the Spirit are opened only when you have said, 'Henceforth I do the will of God rather than my own.'

"In truth, I am the son of God, as you will also be when you have claimed your birthright. If I am unlike you, it is only insofar as one blade of wheat stands higher than another, or as one lamp burns steadfastly while another flickers. You are Andrew's elder brother of the flesh. I am your elder brother of the Spirit.

"When I say to all of you that your souls are eternal, I speak not only of Paradise and the life hereafter, but also of other lives which are long forgotten. Before Simon was, Simon was. Before Andrew was, Andrew was. Yet these brothers in blood shall be enslaved to the world until they become brothers in Spirit, to one another and to every other child of God, by attending closely to the lessons of Heaven and by freely choosing to do the will of Him Who is the Father of us all.

"I call on each of you today to choose joy over misery, freedom over slavery, life over death, and to become the son of God you truly are."

Jesus turned to my beloved and asked, "Philip, why do we call God our Heavenly Father? Why should we not say, our Heavenly Mother?"

Philip was so taken aback by this strange question that for some moments he could not find the words to answer. "Surely God is a man like us, for the Torah tells us the He created Adam in His own image, and all the prophets have called Him Lord."

Jesus smiled and said, "But God created woman as well as man. In whose image was woman created? Man cannot create God. Nevertheless, our forefathers shaped a false vision of God arising from earthly pride, for they would see themselves as gods of this world, with dominion over the fowls of the air, the beasts of the field, and the fish of the sea.

"The things of the Spirit cannot be understood by thinking on the things of this world. Men are the gods of the Earth only through cunning and brute strength. The living God, the Father and Mother of us all, rules not through force but with all-embracing love.

"Therefore, whenever we speak of God our Heavenly Father,

remember that this is nothing more than custom, for God, the eternal Spirit that gives us breath and being, is both man and woman and neither man nor woman. If we are to feel within ourselves even the smallest part of God's glory, we must go beyond all earthly ideas and even beyond words."

When Jesus had gathered all of his disciples into a circle for instruction, he said these things:

"Brothers, remember that the Law of God is written not only on tablets of stone and in the Torah, but in your own hearts as well, and that which is written in your hearts has greater authority than cold words or dusty covenants. Therefore, be not troubled if the Law which the Holy Spirit has graven within your bosom contradicts the Torah, so long as you follow my commandment to love both God and your fellow man.

"It may be that your separate Law, given you by God, is not within the understanding of other men. Therefore, do not trouble their minds or burden their spirits with this seeming paradox, but rest assured that you are in truth a child of God and freely live by your own Law."

Then Jesus said, "But there shall come a time long hence when all hearts shall be opened and everything which is in the soul of man made known. Then it shall be one thousand fold clearer than the light of midday that there is but one Law, and that this Law is eternal and unchanging. In that time of glory all men and all women shall be brothers and sisters, and all hearts and minds joined, for there will be no false or separate understandings of the Law."

When Jesus said this, I thought, "How wondrous it would be to live in that time, when I might tell all men and all women of my love for Philip, and none would condemn or stone me!" But it was only through my earthly ignorance of the truths of the Spirit that I spoke thus, for I did not know then that Jesus was speaking of a time beyond time when the love of God by all would supplant the earthly love that we know here and now.

"Meanwhile," Jesus said, "remember that it is good to follow the Scriptures, but if you study them too closely, you may find in them what is, in truth, not there. The Law was not given to man to provide a livelihood for priests, but to increase understanding and to open the gates of the Kingdom of Heaven to all.

"Therefore, spend more time in listening to the voice of the Holy Spirit within your bosom and looking upon the message written on your own heart, and less in the study of books and the words of learned men who strain at gnats but cannot see the glory of the heavens."

Jesus also spoke to us of joy:

"I tell you that he who would find salvation must first find joy. You should seek this joy in the worship of God, in doing good for others, and in those simple things which God has given you for this earthly life. Do not seek joy in worldly goods, for these are as spoiled fruit or sour wine. But no man can fathom the mystery or splendor of the simple things which God has given.

"Truly, I come to bring joy to all the world, for the worship of our Father is one with joy and one with light. That is why you must be like little children, free of worldly ambition, pride, sin, and the burden of judging others, so that you may feel the endless joy of being a child of God.

"There are those among you who would twist my message and dishonor my teachings for the sake of worldly ambitions, yea, even among you, my beloved disciples. You would make God's worship a thing of long faces and darkness, suffering and sacrifice. But I tell you that no suffering which men may inflict upon you can withstand the power of God's joy, whether they mock you or scourge you or strip you naked and nail you to a cross."

During this time, Jesus taught us how to read the true meaning of his parables.

"The time is come for plain speaking," Jesus said, "I shall unwind the meaning of parables for you, like one who unravels a tangled ball of yarn, laying it all out before you, so that you will not have to ask one another, 'What did he mean when he said that?' For I have not come to bring you riddles or meat for priestly arguments, but to increase the understanding of all.

"Remember first that in my parables I am always speaking of the Spirit and things of the Spirit. Remember also that things of the Spirit are to things of the world of men as day is to night, so that those things which appear to be contradictions may be reconciled, while those which appear to be the same thing may be very different.

"In the parable of the talents, the master of whom I speak is God Himself, and the servants are not two, but legion, since they stand for all the peoples of this Earth. Yet through their actions they are but two kinds of men, the wise and unwise servants.

"In the parable, the master leaves his servants, but in truth it is the other way around. Being in all places at all times, God never leaves anyone. Rather it is His servants who leave Him, when they are born into this world of illusion.

"At the time of each man's and each woman's birth, God bestows special gifts, and indeed there shall come a time long hence when these shall be called 'talents.' These gifts may be for making music or weaving beautiful cloth or healing or giving prophecy.

"Being gifts of the Spirit, these golden talents are not like worldly gifts, for they can be husbanded and increased only by lending them to others, for the glory of God's name and in the service of your fellow man. But he who buries his talents within his own bosom or uses them only to gain power and worldly goods does in truth spend them and waste them, thereby displeasing God."

Then Jesus spoke further of his story of the prodigal son:

"If a son should be away from his birthplace many years, would a father say, 'You may come home only if you take the straightest road'? No. Rather he would sorrow for that child who loses his way or follows twisting paths which lead him still farther from his rightful place. Would not a father rejoice all the more when such a child has found his way at last?

"If God, our Heavenly Father, wants His children with Him, why should He not accomplish this at once, being all-powerful and knowing all? But God is loath to bring His children home in chains, like Roman captives. Rather He waits with loving patience till His children find their way to their Father, out of the fullness of their hearts and love for Him.

"If a child be slow to learn, would a loving father kill him or cast him into darkness? No. Rather the father would cherish him all the more, repeating each lesson many times, till understanding dawns like a rising sun in mind and heart and soul.

"No one may master the lessons of Heaven in a single life, but God, a loving Father, does not decree for His children the fire of eternal damnation. Rather, He repeats His lessons with patience beyond the understanding of men, giving His children all the time they need to learn. This is why I say to you, you must be born again.

"Time after time you will be born of the flesh, but when, after many lives, you have learned the lessons of Heaven, you will be born of the Spirit. From that time on, eternal Paradise is yours."

During this time, Jesus also spoke to us of healing:

"Kings and tyrants may wreak suffering and death upon you, but this is as nothing against the suffering which you inflict upon yourselves, which men call sickness or possession by devils.

"Through your prayers and with your hands, I shall teach you how to heal the sick and cast out devils, but in truth these cures come to pass only through the will of God, when sufferers yield themselves up to His will and His love. For indeed, it is the sufferers themselves who bring the illness to their bodies.

"Men will say that the cures we work are miracles. And so they are, but not as men suppose. For we shall bring comfort to the wretched not with tricks of pagan magic but through the power of God Himself.

"We shall cause those who feel themselves outside the Law to look upon the face of God, for one who has seen the face of God cannot be sick in body or in mind. We shall not impose cures from without by leeches or herbs that make the body burn with fever, but we shall show the sick how they may heal themselves through the glory, love and power of God.

"We shall touch lepers and others whom men call untouchable, summoning forth the power of God which is in every man and woman, and making them whole. We shall make sickness health, sorrow joy, and darkness light."

And so we labored joyfully together in our Father's vineyard, under our beloved Master, going about the countryside from town to town, healing the sick and bringing comfort to the afflicted, praying and laughing, breaking bread together, singing and dancing, and learning wondrous things which Jesus taught us, celebrating the glory of God, and loving all.

## ·IX·

# SIMON AND ANDREW

Shortly after Jesus had blessed the multitude on the mount near Tabgha, Simon said to me, "Come with me, for I must speak with you alone."

The coldness in his voice saddened me, and though it was midday, a shiver touched my very heart. Many times before I had felt Simon's anger, but it was always anger born of love for a younger brother. Now he spoke as he might to someone outside our family and our race as well.

Without turning my head I glanced in Philip's direction. From the concern in his eyes, I knew that he had noticed what was happening between Simon and me, and that he was also troubled. As Simon and I walked away, I could feel Philip's eyes on us, as surely as I could feel the tunic on my own back.

When we were out of sight of Jesus and the others, Simon stopped in the thick of a small grove of trees. I turned toward him, waiting for him to speak further. Instead he raised his arm and struck me so hard with his open hand that I fell to the ground. I picked myself up and looked him in the eye.

"Why have you done this thing, when I have done nothing to you?"

"I did it because I could not bring myself to stone my own brother. I should have done it long ago, but my heart would not believe what my eyes and mind told me was true. You have brought shame upon our father, our mother, and our whole family. You are less than a man."

"How can you call me less than a man, when we have fished side by side since I was a boy twelve years of age?"

"Do you suppose that I am blind? With my own eyes I have seen the unholy lust which you and Philip have for one another. He has lured you into unspeakable sin, as easily as a harlot of Sidon might beguile a simple-minded farm worker."

"How can you say or even think such a thing of Philip? No one among us twelve is more devout. No one has followed the teachings of Jesus more faithfully. Though Philip and I shall love one another unto death and even beyond, you cannot call this sin."

"Is it not sin for a man to sleep with another man? Is it not true that you have slept with Philip, as a real man might sleep with a woman? It turns my stomach to think of it!"

"Yes, we have lain together, but our love for one another is as holy as any love between man and woman."

"One sin that stinks like yours is enough. Will you add blasphemy to it?"

When Simon reviled me so, I would have struck him back, but I knew that meeting anger with anger was against our Master's teachings, so I only said, "Jesus himself has told us that the love which Philip and I have for one another is holy. Since you will not believe your own brother, ask him."

"No! I will not speak to anyone else of our family's shame. You are not fit to utter the name of Jesus, much less to follow him. When we became disciples of Jesus, I gave up my wife, my children, my trade and my home. You have given up nothing. Fall on your knees and beg God's forgiveness for your sin."

"No! I will not ask God's forgiveness for being what God Himself has made me."

"Then leave the company of the disciples and your weaver's son. No longer live among righteous, God-fearing men and women. Go into the desert to fast and scourge yourself. You must atone for your sin."

"No. I will not do that either, for love is not sin."

"If you will not keep God's covenant with his chosen people, then renounce your heritage. Go into some foreign land and take your evil Philip with you. Worship idols. Wear an earring and curl your hair, like some Greek trader who sleeps with Persian camel boys."

"No, I will not forsake the land of my birth, and I will go on following Jesus, as I will go on loving Philip, for I belong to both of them."

Simon spat full in my face. "Since you will not abandon your sin, you are no longer my brother. I disown you! Do not speak to me. Do not look at me. Tell your weaver's son to keep his distance from me, or I will tear him in two as one would rip a rotten piece of cloth."

Simon turned on his heel and left. Though I knew that I had not sinned against God or the teachings of Jesus, I sat on a stone with my head in my hands and wept, for I loved my brother still.

In a little while Philip came to me, as I had known he would. He knelt beside me and lifted up my head. "Then Simon knows that we love one another."

"Yes," I said, "but he does not call it love. He spat in my face and disowned me."

"It rends my heart, knowing that brother has been turned against brother because of your love for me. Should I leave you and return to Bethsaida, never to see you again?"

I got to my feet, lifting Philip at the same time. I held him close and leaned his head against my shoulder. "Pray, do not speak of leaving me! I would rather have my breath leave my body. Without you there is no sun, no joy. My life would be ashes, my body a prison."

"Then what are we to do? Shall we leave together, to seek out some land where a man may love another like himself without shame?"

"No," I answered, "as Jesus has chosen us, we have the right to go on serving him. No man can shame us! The Law which the Holy Spirit has written on our hearts tells us our love is holy. So long as we follow the two commandments of Jesus and our own Law, the Kingdom of God is ours. We cannot sin."

"But what of your brother, Simon?"

"I love my brother dearly, more than I can tell, but Simon's troubles are the children of his own mind. If he does not understand now, he will understand later. If enlightenment does not come in this life, it will come in another life, when he himself shall love another of his own sex."

"But will he not set the other disciples against us?"

"No, Simon will speak to no one of this, not even to Jesus, lest he bring shame to his family and himself. Though he disowns me, I am still his brother in the eyes of all other men."

"Should we tell Jesus what has come to pass?"

"Why should we tell Jesus what he surely knows already? We have no need to speak of this again. Let us love one another and do God's work and live out our lives together."

## ·X·

# THE LAST TEACHING

Shortly before the entry into Jerusalem, Jesus came to Philip and me, saying, "Come, let us walk together."

When we were out of hearing of the others, he said, "There are things which we must speak of, while there is time. Before two Sabbaths have passed I shall be put to death, and we shall not be able to speak apart again."

"This cannot be, Lord," Philip cried, "You could not be put to death unless you willed it."

"I do not will it, nor does God. Nevertheless, I shall not prevent it, for man can be saved only through his own actions and by his own increase in understanding. Though I shall be put to death, I will not die. On the third day I shall rise from the dead, but I will not stay with you for long thereafter. I must return to our Father."

"You also, my beloved disciples, will be put to death in my name, though at different times and in different places."

"How can this be, Lord?" I cried. "You have promised that we two should never be parted, even in death."

"Nor shall you be," Jesus answered. "This is beyond your present understanding, but you must believe."

"Which of us two will die first, Master?" Philip asked. "Will it be I?"

"Yes," Jesus answered, "that is how it will be. Though you have foreseen the deaths of others, you cannot know the hour of your own passing. You will die many years before Andrew."

Like sick children, Philip and I could not staunch our tears and sobbing, so that neither of us could speak. I could not bear up under the burden of knowing that I should have to go on living without the two whom I loved most in all the world. Jesus drew us to his bosom and embraced us, allowing us to give way to our heavy emotions unchecked.

After a short while, he gently pushed us away and said, "Enough of this. Sorrow is but the other face of joy. Unless night falls, the new day cannot dawn. There are many things which we must speak of, while there is time."

I mastered my feelings as best I could and listened.

"First, Andrew, I charge you to remember everything that has passed between us, for false doctrines will be spread in my name, and seeds of judgment, hate and death will be sown by those who call themselves my followers. Also, I have told you things which are not to be given to the world at this time. Yet, when the time is ripe, you will open your heart and bear witness, setting down my true sayings that proclaim God's love for all His children."

"How can that be, Lord," I asked, "seeing that I cannot write?"

"I do not speak of this life, but of another long hence, when you will once again be a lover of men.

"The second thing I would speak of is this: Remember that while God's Law is eternal and unchanging, man sees the Law only dimly, from afar, through the mists of this world of illusion. It may sometimes seem that the Law has changed when in truth the only change has been in the level of man's understanding. For this is the rule: The greater man's understanding, the simpler the Law.

"That is why I have come into the world at this time. Before I came, there were ten commandments and many proscriptions. I have given you two commandments which replace all these: That you should love the Lord thy God with all your heart and with all your soul and with all your mind, and that you should love your neighbor as yourself. If only you keep these two commandments, you cannot sin.

"Do not suppose that I have chosen you twelve because you are the holiest among all living men. Rather, you stand for all men in all stages of spiritual understanding, from John, the most enlightened, to Judas Iscariot, the most misguided. Except for him who shall betray me, future generations will call you all 'blessed' or 'Saint.' This is one of the paradoxes of this world, for nothing could be further from the truth.

"You, Andrew, and you, Philip, are among the closest to my heart. You alone followed the teachings of my messenger, John the Baptist, and you were the first to know me as a true son of God."

"How could we not know that, Master?" said Philip, "seeing that you have given us two a gift even more precious than life itself, and one which no man of this world could bestow?"

Then Jesus placed his right hand on Philip's head and said, "Beloved Philip, you stand next to John, who shall be with me forever in Paradise when this life is done, for you have the loving trust and simple heart of a child of God."

It gladdened me to know that my beloved was so favored of God. Then I asked, "Where stands my brother Simon, Lord?"

Jesus frowned, and my heart sank when he answered: "It is mainly through your brother Simon and another who is not among the twelve that my teachings will be perverted and false doctrine spread throughout the world. Future generations will make more of my death than of my life, more of my sorrows than of my joy.

"Simon will not reap the harvest, but he will sow the seed, not knowing where those things he does with good intent will lead. And people yet unborn will take Simon's greatest weakness to be his greatest strength.

"When I shall have left you a second time, Simon will take for himself the office of head priest, for he is not content to be only a fisher of men but would be a prince of this world. As I have said that the last shall be first, so must it follow that the first shall be last.

"In spite of this, you must still love your brother Simon, as I do. What he does, he does only through lack of understanding and not from want of love for me.

"Because of the nature of men, my coming into the world at this time shall be a tree bearing both fruit and thorns. As I have given you a new covenant, so shall I also give you hypocrites and false priests, for the thirst after power is very strong in men so blinded by the worthless riches of this world that they do not know the joy of being a child of God.

"There are those who will becloud the minds of their brothers and sisters with incense, graven images, and empty words that fall like tinkling brass upon the ear. I am a man, even as you, but they will say that I am very God and that I came into this world as a sacrificial lamb. Indeed, God is within me, and I am truly the son of God, as you are also, yet the Lord our God Who created us all stands alone in majesty. There is none beside Him.

"Though I leave this world, I shall always be with my brothers in Spirit, insofar as they are with me, even to the millennium. But there will arise false priests who claim that they alone are keepers of the word, and that no one may come to God except through them. They will boast of this so loudly and so often that the many will not hear my voice nor the voice of the God and Father of us all. Those few who hear will be called heretics and be put to death.

"Scores, nay, hundreds of worldly temples will be built in my name. The head priests of these temples will dispute among themselves which of them stands for the one true church. The one true church, which is eternal, lives, but do not look for it in houses raised by men who serve the ends of future Caesars in my name. As I have said, the whole world and all the heavens are God's church, can you suppose that man can shut it in with walls?

"Though these are sad tidings, do not despair, dear brothers. At the end of time and beyond time, the love of God in all, by all, for all will still all argument and right all error. Then all men and women will be brothers and sisters, for they will have found their way home."

Jesus turned to me and said, "Remember also my prophecy that brother shall be set against brother in my name. This is because of their separate understandings of the Law."

Then I asked, "Do you mean that Simon and I will be set against one another, Lord?"

"Yes," said Jesus, "that is how it will be. As Simon has disowned you, you must disown his false understanding of the task which I have set out for the twelve. Though he be your elder brother and a second father to you, you and Philip must stand against him, but you shall not stand alone."

As he said this last, his eyes took on that childlike sparkle which I had seen so often in the past when he was speaking in jest. Therefore I asked, "Do you mean that you will be with us in Spirit, Master?"

"Yes, I mean that, but I also mean more than that. When the time comes, you will see."

Our hearts were heavy with the sorrowful things Jesus had told us, yet his face shone with a greater joy and radiance than I had ever seen, as if we had been speaking of the fairest and most pleasant things in Heaven and Earth, so that we were gladdened in spite of ourselves.

"Come, brothers," he said, "no more long faces or tear-rimmed eyes! Remember that the Kingdom of God is always at hand and be joyful! Let us rejoin the others."

## ·XI·

# THIRTY PIECES OF SILVER

How can I speak of Judas Iscariot, who is also a part of the story of Jesus and his followers? If the error belonged to Judas alone, it would be simple. But Judas, being the man he was and doing what he did, caused me to doubt that the Spirit of God moves within all men. I could not love him.

Until Judas joined the disciples, I had never met any man or woman I disliked. Indeed, my brother Simon had often told me that I was far too trusting, as easily taken in as a slow-witted child. Most of my countrymen held that all Romans were oppressors, idolaters and little more than beasts, but once when I was about fifteen years of age, on the way to Philip's house, I had fallen in with a Roman soldier named Lucullus. He told me how much he missed his wife and his son who was almost my age, and how he longed to be home once more, tending his own garden in peace, far from swords and spears and marching troops and barracks life.

When I told Simon of this chance meeting and said that Lucullus must be a good man and a loving husband and father, Simon looked at me in wonderment. "A good man? A thief and murderer would be more to the point! If you were a minnow, you would soon make a tasty meal for a bigger fish!"

When I set eyes on Judas Iscariot, I understood for the first time what it meant to hate. My very skin prickled, as if I were covered with crawling flies or beetles.

Of all the followers of Jesus, Judas was the only one whom Jesus had not called to himself. When Judas came to the encampment at Cana to ask whether he might join the other disciples, Jesus said only, "Yes. I have been awaiting you."

Judas was not an ill-favored man. Indeed, judged by the cast of his features alone, he was handsome in a dark way, with shining teeth as white as alabaster and a nose as straight as a Roman's. During his years with us, I saw many women look at him in lust, as I had seen him return their looks. Yet I pitied any woman who might lie with him, for his heart was flint.

There was something in the man which set my teeth on edge. When he was asked a question he never answered straight off but thought a while, as if choosing those words his listener wanted to hear rather than what he truly felt. A shudder went through me whenever I heard him speak loving words, seeing that his eyes were filled with hate.

When Judas joined us, all that he told us of himself was that he had been one of the Zealots. I could not believe this. The Zealots were what they were, not counting the cost, while Judas was a man of stealth.

Once I fell into conversation with a fellow townsman of Judas who had come to hear Jesus. He told me that Judas was a son of a woman of the town. His father was said to be a rich landowner who would not recognize a son born out of wedlock. Therefore Judas hated all people because they shunned him and scorned his mother. And Judas had sworn that he would gain more power than all the other citizens of his town, so that one day he might return to take his vengeance on them.

From time to time, Judas would urge Jesus to use his power to overthrow the Romans, but not in the open way my brother Simon had urged at Capernaum. Rather, Judas would say that one of us should become a servant to a member of the Sanhedrin, or that we should send a beautiful woman to entice a Roman commander, with an eye to learning their plans.

Once, when Judas counseled our Master in this way, Jesus said, "Let the Romans and the high priest do what they will. Why should we covet earthly kingdoms when all the Kingdom of Heaven is ours?"

A few months after Judas had joined the disciples, I said to Philip, "I do not like Judas Iscariot, nor do I trust him."

"No more do I."

"He talks so much of spies that I have come to think he himself must be a spy in the service of the Romans or the high priest."

"That makes sense," Philip said. "In my bones I feel that you have guessed the truth. Should we not speak of this to Jesus?"

When next we were able to speak to Jesus alone, I said, "Master, I fear that Judas Iscariot is no child of God but a spy working for the high priest or the Romans."

"You are both correct and mistaken. Judas is an agent of the high priest. Indeed, when the time comes he will deliver me into the hands of the Romans, that I might be put to death. Yet Judas is also a child of God."

"This cannot be," I cried, "that a child of God should betray the very son of God! If he does this ungodly thing, I shall avenge you!"

"No vengeance will be taken, but the wrong will be righted."

"Who will right it?" I asked.

"Judas himself, though this will take many lifetimes. Whatever Judas does, you must not hate him, lest one error become two, for this is the way of the world. Remember what I have told you: that no one may harm the son of God, whose soul is beyond harm. I command you to love Judas, for no man has more need of love."

While I had always tried to follow the teachings of our Master, this was the one time when I could not do what he asked. Being a man, I could not love Judas.

That last night in the garden, Judas could have pointed out our Lord to the Romans. He chose instead to deliver Jesus with a kiss. This was his way, to twist a show of love into a tool of betrayal and death.

When the Roman soldiers rushed toward Jesus, my brother Simon was so enraged that he snatched from its scabbard a dagger worn by one of the Roman guards. Slashing out blindly, Simon cut off the tip of the soldier's left ear. Seeing this, another soldier cried out, "Seize that Jew also. He has attacked a soldier of the Emperor."

In an instant Jesus had touched the ear of the wounded soldier and made it whole again, the blood vanishing from his neck and tunic.

"Let my brother go," Jesus said. "Surely you have dreamed this. You can see that the man is unharmed."

The soldier whom Simon had wounded looked about in astonishment. Clearly he saw that no man could do what Jesus had done. He would not lay a hand on our Master, but fled into the night instead.

When the Roman captain flung the bag of coins to Judas, I saw at last that Jesus had spoken truly when he said that Judas had acted as he did only through ignorance. Now that Jesus was in the custody of the Romans, Judas understood that he had fallen into the gravest error ever committed by man. The look of hate and pride was gone forever from his eyes, now opened to the horror of his own deeds. He gave a cry more animal than human and, like the wounded soldier healed by Jesus, fled into the night.

I could forgive the Roman soldier who had bound the wrists of Jesus. I could forgive the two who walked to his right and left. I could forgive even the Roman captain who marched before him. They did not know what they were doing.

But what of one who had followed Jesus for years, feeling his presence, hearing the words of the son of God, seeing his acts of mercy toward the afflicted, the homeless, and oppressed? I could not forgive Judas, much less love him.

## ·XII·

# THE CRUCIFIXION

Would that I had never lived to see that day! Philip and I harbored the secret hope that Jesus would not suffer them to put him to death but would use God's power to save himself and to reveal to both Jew and Roman who he was, so that all would fall down and worship him. Yet, when I saw him bent beneath the weight of the cross, his brow pierced by thorns, struggling up the steep way to the Place of the Skull, mocked, humiliated, and scourged, I knew this would not be. Then both Philip and I buried our heads in our hands and cried, "Oh, Lord! Oh, Lord! Would it were I instead!"

If there had been only moaning and lamentations, it would have been more bearable, but for the crowd this was a holiday, a bloody pagan celebration. Roman officers in shining armor and scarlet capes strutted like peacocks. Knots of the high priest's followers laughed and cried out, "Hail, Jesus of Nazareth, King of the Jews!" Vendors hawked their wares, and citizens of every class gaped open-mouthed at the spectacle, as if they would catch flies thereby. The scuffling of so many feet raised clouds of dust that nearly stopped the breath.

Through the crowd we caught sight of John comforting Mary, the mother of Jesus. He cradled her head against his shoulder and spoke words of comfort to her. We marveled that in this carnival of death he could be so loving and so steady of purpose. Then we remembered how Jesus had told us that John was so pure in Spirit that he would be forever in Paradise after this earthly life.

We sorrowed for our Master, yet we knew he could not truly die, but would rise again from the dead, as he himself had prophesied. We sorrowed more for these stupid, cruel animals who called themselves men. Could they not see what they were doing to themselves? For they were putting to death the only one who could show them the path to salvation.

We stumbled along to the crest of Golgotha with the crowd, but neither Philip nor I witnessed the raising of the cross or the death of our Lord. When a Roman soldier held a spike over the wrist of that blessed arm which had wrought so many miracles, while another soldier raised a heavy mallet to drive it home, I fell to the ground in a dead faint.

It was a long time before I came to myself again, and even then I lay on the ground in a crumpled heap, lacking the will to move, deaf to the cruel gibes of Jew and Roman, numb to the careless kicks of passers-by.

Even after the darkness came down and torrents of rain flailed the streets, driving away the mocking crowd, I lay there like one dead.

Philip had not fainted, but had drawn away from the crowded square into an alleyway, for the horror of that scene had made him retch. Then for a long time, as he later told me, he had sat on a stone, like one who had been struck a blow on the head, hardly knowing what was happening, or even who he was.

Shortly after the rain began, Philip came to his senses, summoned up his strength as best he could, and came to me. He helped me to my feet. We were sore ashamed at our weakness, for if we had been able to endure this bitter cup without flinching, we might have ministered to the needs of our beloved Master in his last hour. Yet it was our deep and abiding love for him that had undone us. We hung our heads in shame and sorrow, for we could not bear to turn our eyes toward the cross on which our master hung.

"Andrew," Philip said, "let us leave this place of horrors, for this is the blackest day the world has ever seen, since God first created the world."

"Truly it is," I replied. "The forces of darkness in the souls of men have put out the light of the world. Yet Jesus himself has said that the night of this black day shall bring the dawn of a new age with a new covenant. We must live in that promise, and do God's work, and love one another."

Our hearts had been wrenched from our bosoms by the pain and horror of what had passed here. We were so weak that we could hardly stand alone, much less walk, and so we helped each other along, with our arms around one another's shoulders, stumbling on the slippery cobblestones like drunken men, half-blind with tears and the pelting rain, I covered with bruises, my tunic and robe clotted with mud, and Philip still reeking of his own vomit.

We never once looked back toward the crest of Golgotha, nor ever passed that way again.

# ·XIII·

# A PARTING OF BROTHERS

After our Master had left us for the second time to return to his Father and ours, all but one of the remaining followers of Jesus were gathered together in the upper room, John being with Mary, the mother of Jesus. We were bereft that our Master was no longer among us in the flesh, though he had promised that he would always be with us in Spirit.

I felt sorrow and confusion in my heart, as I thought back on the last time that Jesus had spoken alone with Philip and me. I knew that Philip felt as I did and supposed that the others shared some of our doubts and fears.

"What shall we do, Andrew, now that our shepherd is no longer among us?" Philip asked.

I could not answer his question, for I did not know, being a lost sheep also. We were not rabbis, only the simple followers of the one great Rabbi.

Then Simon said, "We must make plans, so that the teachings of our Lord may live and flourish. Rome is the seat of all power, so it should also be our new Jerusalem and the seat of our church. We must make our way thence, though this will take many years. We shall preach and build temples in towns and cities all along the way. These may be small at first, but they will grow in size and glory and celebrate the name of Jesus."

Levi the tax collector was the first to agree, saying, "That is a good plan. But first we must build a treasury, so that we may have the wherewithal to do good works."

"Surely we ought not to do these things," I said. "What need have we of plans? From day to day we will be told by the Holy Spirit within us where we should go and what we should do. What need have we of worldly treasures when all the treasures of Heaven itself are ours? What need have we of churches? Would Jesus have us raise temples to celebrate his name when he himself has said that he was a man, very like us? The whole world is God's temple, and Jesus has said it is enough whenever two or three should come together in God's name."

Having known Simon all my life, I could see that he was enraged at hearing his younger brother question his authority. Still, he would not give vent to his anger in the presence of the others. Therefore he spoke softly, with a show of fatherly concern. "You have a man's body, Andrew, yet you are a child and ignorant in the ways of the world. We must do all these things, and we must also decide how we shall choose those disciples who will follow us. Would you defy your elder brother who has been a father to you?"

"I will in this," I answered, "for it is against our Rabbi's teachings. We have only one leader, and he has said there is no first among us, neither younger nor elder. We are all equals."

As Simon had disowned me, I had supposed that he would gladly be rid of Philip and me, that he might no longer need to suffer our company. Now I saw that, although my brother looked upon me as a dimwitted child and a godless sinner, he loved me still, and my heart was heavy for both of us.

His brows drew together in anger, a look that I had often seen while yet a stripling, and when he spoke next his voice thundered. "Truly, you are a simpleton. Would you bring down all that our Lord has worked and died for by not doing those things which any prudent servant would do? Would you dream away the teachings of Jesus and bury your talents?"

"No, I would never do that," I answered, "but I will honor the commands of the Holy Spirit within my bosom and follow in the foot-steps of Jesus himself, even if this should mean that I must defy you who have been a second father to me."

"Then we have come to a parting of the ways, though we be brothers in blood as well as in the service of our Lord. Philip has followed your lead in all else. Will he follow you in this?"

"Yes," said Philip, "I will go with Andrew, for he is a true servant of God and speaks my own heart."

At first I thought that Philip and I should have to stand alone against all the others, but there were two who drew apart from Simon and Levi and the others, coming to stand beside us. Then Nathaniel, also called Bartholomew, put his arm about my shoulder, and Labbaeus, also called Jude, put his about Philip's shoulder.

Nathaniel was the next to speak: "I too see no need for plans, or treasuries, or for building temples of worship, for walls shut out far more than they enclose."

As Nathaniel spoke, I remembered the last teaching of Jesus, when he had told Philip and me that we two should not stand alone against all the rest, and was glad.

I could see that Simon was surprised that Nathaniel and Labbaeus, as well as Philip and I, should defy him. As we turned to leave, he said, "If you must go, though what you do is wrong, then go in peace."

Nathaniel, Labbaeus, Philip, and I left together, and never saw our brothers again.

## ·XIV·

# THE FIRST MISSION

The four of us were saddened that the flock of Jesus had thus been scattered, first by treason and death and then by the falling out of brothers. Still, each of us knew that he had the love of the other three, and that we were doing the will of our Master. Henceforth his teachings would be our food and drink, our refuge from all doubts and fears.

Our parting from our brothers brought the four of us closer together than we had ever been before, so that I was bold enough to ask what I would not have asked until this time: "Nathaniel, what is it that I see in your eyes whenever you look upon Labbaeus?"

Nathaniel smiled, "Surely you of all men know the answer. Is it not the same thing I see in your eyes when you look upon Philip?"

Then the four of us laughed and embraced one another, seeing that we were brothers in more ways than one. Until this time Philip and I had thought we were the only two in all of Israel like ourselves, and Nathaniel and Labbaeus had supposed the same of themselves. We all gave thanks for the mercy of God, and for the wisdom of Jesus, who had shown us that one man may love another without sin.

After this, Nathaniel said, "It would be pleasant, Brothers, to share our labors and to work side by side in our Father's vineyard, but there is so much to be done and so little time that I fear this cannot be, for we must bring the good news of the teachings of

Jesus to as many as we can. Does it seem meet to you that the two of us and the two of you should part and come together once more at Passover here in Jerusalem, in memory of our Lord?"

"This seems very meet," I said, "for then we might greet one another and speak of our missions and celebrate the resurrection of our Lord together."

And so said Philip and Labbaeus.

"Which way will you go, Brothers?" I asked.

"We shall go to the east," Nathaniel said, "and whither you?"

"We shall go to the north," I answered, for this was what the Holy Spirit told me at that time.

When Philip and I set out together, sometimes our teachings fell on fertile ground and sometimes on sand, but all in all this was a joyous season.

Whenever we stopped, the little children would be drawn to Philip like bees to flowers or moths to flame. Then he would give them little winks and make funny faces and tell them little stories in a hundred different voices, croaking like a frog or quacking like a duck. And the children's laughter would tinkle like little bells in the wind.

In this way, without saying so in words, Philip showed them that joy is part and parcel of worship and the Law, and I was glad, for I knew that their whole lives thereafter would be better for this.

In the beginning, the village elders would make long faces and shake their heads at seeing Philip do these things. From their understanding of the Law, it was not meet that a grown man and a messenger of God should behave in these childish ways. But soon the elders would be laughing in spite of themselves, and would understand that Philip was truly holy. I was glad of this as well, for I knew that their own lives would also be better thereby.

Whenever we came to a new village, the elders would welcome me as if I were a very wise man, calling me "Rabbi." In the beginning I was so shamed by this that I would blush and feel that I should own to being merely an ignorant fisherman who could neither read nor write. Soon I came to understand that this feeling of shame on my part was but the other face of vanity and earthly pride, and that I gave too much weight to trifles and too little to the power of the living water of God's word. For I had been the first student of the greatest teacher, the only teacher, and he spoke through me.

Also, I understood that through the power of Jesus and the grace of God, I had in truth become the "Rabbi" that men called me. Neither could any earthly scholar know what I knew, nor any earthly physician work the cures I did. Their knowledge came of this world, where mine was of the Kingdom of Heaven, for I had seen the face of God and understood the Law which was beyond theirs, the Law of God's love which binds us to Him and to all our brothers and sisters. And Jesus himself had given me the gift of healing, through my prayers and in my hands. All these things made me feel joyful and chosen and humble.

Whenever we could, Philip and I shared our minds and our hearts and our bed, as well as our work in our Father's vineyard. This could not always be, for we could not refuse the hospitality of our brothers to whom we brought the message of salvation. Some would have us stay with them forever, if we would.

One night when we were alone together, out of the sight and hearing of all other men, I twirled a lock of Philip's beard about my finger and said, "How beautiful you are! Truly you are a child of God. You are more beautiful than ripening wheat in the wind, or the first unfolding of the lily, or the shining waters of Galilee at dawn. Your hands weave broken threads of life into a tapestry of love. You are my first and my last, my going out and my coming in, for I love you more than life itself."

Then Philip wept for joy and said, "Neither man nor woman ever had a lover such as you, Andrew, nor one more devoted to God."

So we spent many loving nights together, under the new moon and full moon, in heat and cold, lovers as well as fellow workers in our Father's vineyard.

## ·XV·

# A CHANCE MEETING

It was late summer. The day was as dry as charred wood, the midmorning sun already white-hot. Insects buzzed and clacked and chirped in the parched bush. Small birds darted from stalk to stalk.

Philip and I were following a dusty path leading north. We might have been the only human beings on earth. There was no sign of a town, a house, a vineyard, or a field for growing grain – only earth, sky, scorched grass, and the smaller creatures of God's Kingdom.

We were walking along, laughing and singing songs we had known since our childhood, my arm about Philip's shoulder and his around my waist. Presently we came to a crossroad. Looking to his left, Philip cried out, "Surely this cannot be!"

I looked that way also and saw far up the road a solitary figure walking toward us. It was none other than John, the brother of James, our one-time partner in fishing, and the most favored disciple of our Lord. Philip and I hailed him and ran to meet him.

What a joyous reunion! We laughed and embraced all around, clapping each other on the shoulder, the three of us talking at once.

Studying John's face, I recalled how Jesus had said that John surpassed all of the other disciples in understanding. I saw that his features had not changed in the slightest, yet he looked different. He was more joyful than I had ever known him to be before, a seeker who had found the answers to all his questions. And when I looked directly into his eyes, I knew that he, like Jesus, had become a true son of God.

"How do you come to be so far from Nazareth?" I asked. "We had supposed that you would still be with Mary, the mother of Jesus."

"Mary has joined her son in Paradise," John answered. "Hers was the happiest passing ever known, for Jesus was with us at the end, assuring her eternal peace and cradling her in his arms, as she had once cradled him."

"And whither are you going now?"

"Like you, I go wherever the Holy Spirit leads me, making no plans but doing the will of God from day to day."

"When did you last see your brother James and my brother Simon?"

"I saw them not more than a fortnight ago," John replied.

"And how fares my brother?"

"He is well and finds great joy in his mission. Now he knows that it is much better to be a fisher of men than a man who fishes. Whenever he preaches people come from miles around to hear him, for no living follower of Jesus is more persuasive than Simon."

"And are you one with them in their mission?"

"I am one with all my brothers and sisters. Still, I cannot join Simon and James and the others in their mission nor teach the things they do, for their understanding of the lessons of Jesus differs from mine."

"Then what things are they teaching?" I asked.

"They say that God sent Jesus into the world to be sacrificed, as an atonement for the sins of all. They say that we may win salvation only if we believe in Jesus as the only begotten son of God and the Messiah. Further, they say that we will suffer hellfire and eternal damnation unless we do this forthwith, in this very lifetime, for each man and woman has only a single lifetime.

"Also, they preach that doomsday is upon us, which shall be the end of the world, when the dead shall rise from their graves, and God and Jesus shall come in glory to judge the living and the dead, casting into eternal darkness all unbelievers."

"Surely they are mistaken in this!" Philip cried.

"I would not call them mistaken, for they do these things in the hope that they can thereby hasten the coming of the Kingdom of God. There are many paths to Heaven and many steps along the way. Some who will not hear the lessons of Jesus as you or I would teach them are open to the message of Simon and his followers. This can be the beginning of understanding."

"To my mind," I said, "this would seem to mean that those who follow Simon feel that they are one with each other, but not with those who turn a deaf ear to their message."

"That is true." John replied, "Although they are mistaken in this, the error will be righted in time. One day the peoples of every corner of the world will know that we are all one, as we are all children of God."

"Do you miss your brother James?" I asked.

"Yes, he is always in my thoughts, and I miss him very much, but I should miss him even more if all men and women were not my brothers and sisters.

"We have talked enough of these things – let us speak of you. It gladdens me to see that you find such happiness in your mission and so much pleasure in one another's company. When Jesus said that we should love one another, perhaps he did not know that the two of you would take his teaching so much to heart."

I blushed and Philip laughed, saying, "Indeed, Jesus knew this from the beginning, when he first met Andrew and before I had ever set eyes on our Master. He has told us that we may love one another without sin and that we shall never be parted, even in death."

"You do not condemn our earthly love for one another?" I asked John.

"Far from condemning you, I am happy for you," John answered. "In this lifetime I have lain with neither woman nor man, for I love all men and all women as brothers and sisters. Yet I know that in other lives I myself have been both man and woman, and I have loved my own sex as well as the other. The love of man for man is a step along the way, just as the love of man for woman is."

"Will you not join us a while?" I asked. "Then we could talk of old times in Bethsaida and work together in our Father's vineyard."

"Nothing would give me greater happiness, but the Holy Spirit tells me that I must press on. I will walk with you as far as the next village, but there we must part once more."

## ·XVI·

# THE VISIT

One evening, shortly before Rosh Hashanah, after we had encamped for the night, Philip and I were seated on the ground talking together. Suddenly a light appeared before us, no farther than the stature of a man from where we sat. It grew in brightness till it seemed as if the sun had come to earth, so that we had to shield our eyes with our hands. Knowing this to be a miracle, we rose to our feet. As the light faded, Jesus stood before us. Still we could not speak, being struck dumb, like men who have no wits about them.

Then Jesus smiled and said, "Have you lost your tongues? Is this how you greet an old friend, with silence? Must you, like Thomas, touch me to assure yourselves that I am real?"

"No, Lord," I answered, "we have no doubt of that, yet we are amazed. While we always feel your presence through the Holy Spirit, we have not seen you these many months. Thence, it must be that what you come to tell us is a thing of great importance."

"You are right," said Jesus. "I have come to remind you that there is much to do and little time. Along the path you have been following, shortly beyond this place, is a fork in the road. When you reach it, Philip shall take the path to the right, and you, the path to the left."

"No!" I cried. "How can you ask this thing of us? Surely we can fulfill our mission working together. Since you have said that

Philip shall die many years before I do, how can I know if we should part, whether or not he might be put to death?"

"Having no gift for prophecy, you cannot know," Jesus answered. "Yet you do know that life is eternal and death an illusion. I have assured you many times that this is so. My standing here before you now is proof.

"Though I have told you that your love for Philip, and Philip's love for you, is holy, you must not lose your souls in the love of the body. For many men and women, the love of the body is the highest rapture that they know on earth. Yet the love of the body is but the merest shadow of the true love of the Spirit, one thousandth of a thousandth part, as the light of a single lamp is to the sun. You yourself have caught some glimmer of that truth on this, your first mission."

"I would not disobey you, Master," I said, "but surely Philip and I can best accomplish the tasks which you have set for us if we work together, since Philip shows the little children that your way is joy, while I instruct the elders in your truth. Without Philip I am but half a man."

"Have you become a hypocrite and a false servant," asked Jesus, "that you would seek to find holes in the Law which you might slip through, so that you may serve your earthly pleasures? I ask no sacrifice of you, my brothers, only that you forsake a lesser joy to find one greater."

Then Philip, who had not spoken before this, said: "Andrew, it rends my heart to hear you dispute our Lord's commands. This is the very son of God. He is the one who has freed us of men's opinions, that we might love one another without sin. He has returned our very souls to us, leading us out of darkness into light and giving us the peace and joy of Heaven. Therefore, let us do this little thing he asks of us."

Jesus spoke again: "The choice is yours alone to make, Andrew, but Philip counsels you wisely. Though the final lesson is always the hardest, do not protest. This is the lesson for which you have lived this life."

Then Jesus spread his arms and said, "Come, my beloved brothers, embrace me once more, as I must take my leave."

When Jesus had left as he had come, I said to Philip, "Can you have such meager love for me, to call our parting a thing of no consequence, knowing that we may never again in this lifetime see one another?"

And Philip answered, "Dear Andrew, remember that even death shall have no power to part us, so great our love for one another is. Jesus himself has promised this. I love you more than the beating of my own heart or my very breath, but I could not love you so much unless I had still greater love for the will of God and the teachings of Jesus.

"As we have loved each other all our lives, even before we knew that such a love could be, wherefore should we speak sharply to one another now? Come, lover of my soul, make love to me."

When Philip spoke thus, I could no longer harden my heart against him, for he had made me see that I had acted like a willful child frightened by shadows cast against the wall.

I threw myself into his waiting arms and clutched him to me, giving him kiss after kiss and vowing never to raise my voice to him again. Cradling my beloved in my arms, I carried him beneath the trees, where we had spread our traveling robes to make a bed.

Since that first night in Capernaum, our joy in one another had grown like the waxing moon. This night our rapture knew no limit, until it seemed less earthly love than love of the Spirit. We were one body, one mind, one heart, one soul.

The following morning when we reached the fork in the road, we wept with joy on parting, Philip taking the path to the right, and I, the path to the left.

On the first full moon after the Feast of Dedication, I began retracing my steps in the direction of Jerusalem, in order that I might be there by the time of Passover, hoping to fall in with Philip somewhere along the way.

The first night after this I awakened flushed with fever and sobbing, for I had dreamed that Philip, like our Lord, had been crucified, dying in agony, and with his life's last breath had called my name. I remembered the prophecy of Jesus and knew that this was no dream but that which had truly come to pass.

I could no longer sleep, but wandered about the countryside to no purpose, now here, now there, tearing my hair and rending my garments. In my great loss, I lost my faith as well, crying: "Lord! How can this be? You have promised that we two should never part, even in death. Why have you forsaken your children, who loved you and trusted in you and followed in your footsteps?"

So I continued all that night, past sunrise, and all the next day, neither preaching nor healing nor doing any other useful thing, until late the following night, when my legs would carry me no farther, so that I dropped in the grass beside the road and fell into a restless sleep.

Then, in another dream, Philip came to me and lay beside me and kissed me full on the lips, saying: "Beloved Andrew, could I ever leave you, even in death? Be of good cheer, and know that what our Lord has promised he will do, for I shall be beside you every moment, waking or sleeping, and in your heart."

Now I understood that Philip had been with me all the while, but that my selfish grief had closed my heart to his presence, because I had doubted God's mercy and denied His will. I was filled with such a sense of Philip's voice and touch and being that we were one. From that time on I knew the peace of the Spirit and never lusted after any other man.

And though in life he had followed my lead in all things but one, now it was I who waited upon Philip, for it was not the Holy Spirit but Philip himself who guided my footsteps, telling me where I should go and what I should do, giving me comfort whenever I despaired and loving me always.

In the week before Passover I arrived in Jerusalem and went to the appointed place. The next day Nathaniel arrived alone, for he and Labbaeus had also been told by Jesus that they should part, this too happening about the time of Rosh Hashanah. So great was our joy at seeing one another that I would not burden Nathaniel's spirit nor rend his heart by telling him of Philip's death.

The following day Labbaeus arrived. After we had greeted one another and embraced, he said, "Come, Andrew, let us sit awhile together, for I bring the heaviest and most sorrowful news that a fellow disciple could give to his brother, and my heart is torn."

"We need not do so," I said, "for I already know what you would tell me: that Philip has been crucified. All this has come to me in a dream on the very night of the day when he died. Do not mourn for me, my brothers, for our beloved Master had promised that Philip and I should never part, even in death, and it is so. He is beside me and within my heart at every moment, even as we speak, and I am joyful."

Then we three embraced again, thanking God for His mercy.

## ·XVII·

# THE LATER MISSIONS

As Jesus had foretold, I lived for many years after Philip's death, growing old in God's service but remaining young in spirit through His grace. I went on, traveling from place to place, preaching and healing and bringing the joyous tidings of the new covenant. I visited many foreign lands, for the Holy Spirit, through Philip, had given me the gift of tongues, that I might carry God's message to Gentile as well as to Jew.

I comforted men and women, young and old, rich and poor. I also led into the light those who lived in darkness and felt themselves outside the Law because they loved another of their own sex, for I could see into their souls. I helped them to understand that they, like all other men and women, are children of God, so that they might love without shame and follow God and be joyful. While I did all these things, I could never charm the little children as Philip had done, for I lacked his grace and childlike spirit.

Having the constant guidance and fellowship of Philip, I gathered no disciples about me. For the voice of Philip within my bosom had counseled me that the Holy Spirit would send me those disciples that I should need.

Levi, the first of these followers, came to me about the time of the Feast of Dedication, one year after Philip's death, and said: "Rabbi, I would follow and serve you, for I would learn of the sayings and miracles of Jesus, and of his life and death and resurrection."

From his speech, I knew that he, like Jesus, was a Nazarene, though we were far from Galilee, and I wondered how he had come to leave his family and friends.

"You are a long way from Nazareth, the town that was the home of Jesus," I said. At this, his mouth dropped open, for he was very young and did not understand that every word he uttered proclaimed his origins.

"You must be a very wise and holy man," he said. "Yes, I am a Nazarene. That is how I first came to know of Jesus. When I was yet a child he often spoke to me and to the other children of Nazareth. Even now, some of the family of Jesus say that he was a man possessed by devils, and that he has brought disgrace upon their name, but I believe him to be the holiest man who ever lived."

I marveled that the newcomer was very like to Philip. He was some two years younger than Philip had been on that day beside the shore of Galilee when first I knew I loved him.

"If you will," I answered, "you may follow me, and I shall teach you all I know of Jesus. Yet you will serve not me but God, for we shall be fellow workers in our Father's vineyard."

At our first meeting, I knew that Levi was also a lover of men, for I had read his heart, but the spirit of Philip told me that the time was not yet ripe to speak of this.

On the Sabbath after he had come to me, Levi threw himself at my feet and kissed the hem of my robe, crying out, "Rabbi, I would not leave you! You are the holiest and wisest man that I have known, yet I am not fit to serve God or to follow Jesus, for I am unclean."

Then I reached down and raised Levi up and embraced him, saying, "As Jesus has commanded us to love God and one another, can love be unclean? Though you love another man, you are a child of God. Know that I also love one of our own sex, for my beloved was Philip, second most favored disciple of our Lord, who was crucified in his name, and who dwells with him now in Paradise, and in my own heart.

"What is the name of him you love?" I asked.

"Joshua," Levi answered, marveling that I had read his heart, and that two disciples of Jesus could have been lovers as well as servants of God.

"Then go to Joshua," I said, "and tell him that you love him. After that, bring him to me, for we three shall be fishers of men together. I shall not be in this place, for it is God's will that I travel on, but the Holy Spirit will guide you to me."

"Surely I cannot do this thing, Rabbi. Being a devout Jew, Joshua will spit in my face and curse me. Since he is older than I, soon his father will arrange for his betrothal. It would be better to let him marry, in the hope that I may be like a second father to his children and share his happiness in them."

"That would be very wrong," I said, "for Joshua returns your love. Even now he feels scorned and rejected, supposing that you fled from Nazareth because you had read his heart and judged him a godless sinner. Be assured that this is true. The spirit of Philip within my bosom has told me so.

"So long as you love in God's name, your love for one another is holy. God has made both you and Joshua what you are, and He has sent you to me that I might lighten your burden. Therefore, go to Joshua and tell him of your love for him. Then, rejoin me once more, and the three of us shall be fellow workers in our Father's vineyard."

Tears of joy ran down Levi's cheeks. He spoke so fast that his words tumbled over one another, saying that his soul which he had lost had been returned to him, and that he had never known such peace and gladness. He blessed God, Jesus and Philip and me as well.

And so it came to pass that Joshua, Levi and I followed together in the footsteps of Jesus. For two full years they remained with me while I taught them all I knew of the sayings and miracles of Jesus. We went from town to town, casting nets for the souls of men, healing the sick, giving comfort to those who sorrowed, and showing those who felt themselves outside the Law that they are children of God.

After this, I told Joshua and Levi that the time had come for us to part, that we might share the good news Jesus had brought to the world with more of our brothers and sisters who dwelled in darkness. They were saddened at our parting but understood that I was speaking truly when I told them that I had taught them everything I knew. My own heart was heavy also, for they had become like sons to me, yet I was glad, knowing that they would serve God faithfully, bringing comfort and joy to many and carrying the message of salvation to all they met.

So long as we lived, Nathaniel, Labbaeus and I met in memory of the resurrection of our Lord, but not in every year nor always in Jerusalem. One year when we met at Capernaum, I remembered that first night I ever spent in Philip's arms and knew that, of all men, I was the most fortunate.

From time to time the three of us would hear that Simon and his followers had built a church in one place or another, calling themselves the only true followers of Jesus and saying that anyone who would find salvation must follow their teachings. For our part, we reared no churches, yet we were content, for we knew that we were following in the footsteps of Jesus, doing our Master's work as he would do it.

And though I died in pain and humiliation, stripped naked and nailed to a cross head down, I died in joy. For my holy Master and Philip were there beside me all the while, and in my heart, saying, "Beloved Andrew, you shall be with us in Paradise today!"

By the grace and mercy of God and through our blessed Lord Jesus, Philip and I were the first two ever to know that a man who loves another man may love and serve God as well, not hiding from the right hand what the left hand does, but in the full light of God's truth, for all things are possible in love.

# PART TWO

## COMMENTARIES ON *THE BOOK OF ANDREW* BY THE AUTHOR AND THE EDITOR

# THE BOOK OF ANDREW:
# A PERSONAL HISTORY

By Charles C. Lehman

You've just finished *The Book of Andrew*, the book I never planned to write, the story that took me by surprise. I did not start with the first word on page one and proceed in a neat, straight-forward manner to the end. Much of the story came to me in isolated, random episodes, which I experienced as emotion-laden images of varying clarity. Since I am not a professional writer, clothing these naked images and emotions in words required a great deal of conscious effort.

There is an exception to this pattern: Most of the words attributed to Jesus came to me just as I have set them down. I did not "hear" these words, but without my bidding they would suddenly fill my mind, just as a long-forgotten song from childhood might crop up unexpectedly. During the three-week period when I worked most intensively on the book, I often woke up at four a.m. with an entire "lesson" in my head.

Though the actual writing of the book started in the summer of 1977, in retrospect it seems that there was a much longer incubation period, when I gradually became aware that personal experiences verging on the bizarre can have a compelling immediacy.

## My First Mystery

The first of the strange happenings that thoroughly shook up my conceptions of reality occurred in the early nineteen sixties. One morning, when I was still half-asleep, the first news item I heard on my clock radio announced that floods in East Pakistan had killed an estimated 100,000 people and left perhaps as many as one million homeless.

When I mentioned this catastrophe to co-workers at my office, it turned out that no one else had heard that particular news story. I searched through every page of the *New York Times* for the next three or four days, without finding any reference to floods in East Pakistan.

After a while, I dismissed this mystery news report as a waking dream, *but some two years later it materialized as a genuine news story, even to the numbers I had heard.*

This seemed an utterly pointless experience. If there is such a thing as precognition, what earthly good is it if no time frame is provided? Nevertheless, this experience did convince me that our minds may occasionally transcend both conscious awareness and our five senses.

## More of the Unexplainable

My personal encounters with precognition have been limited to this single instance, but some years later other unexplainable things began happening. Around 1970, I was passing a church on the West Side of New York City and knew that *I had to go in.* This was not simply an inner compulsion: I felt as if I were being physically pushed into that church. It was my understanding at the time that I should have to go in only once, but I started attending every Sunday and was soon asked to become a vestryman.

Until this happened I had not been a regular churchgoer for some twenty years, mainly because the teachings of the Church made it seemingly impossible to be both gay and religious. In my youth I had alternated between periods of unrepentant promiscuity, when I never set foot inside a church, and periods of deep religiosity, when I attended faithfully and suffered from intense depression over attraction to my own sex. This vacillation between the spiritual and physical was so wearying that I was forced into the self-admission that I *am* gay and that I have always been gay, so I stopped going to church altogether.

The curious nature of my reintroduction to the Church convinced me that God didn't care whether I was homosexual or heterosexual. It also suggested that the Holy Spirit has a sense of humor, something I had never imagined before. It was as if God had taken a leaf from Mark Twain's notebook by saying, "Reports of My death have been greatly exaggerated."

## JUST WHAT IS HOLY, ANYWAY?

Soon, the themes of sexuality and religion began to merge. A Bach fugue could be a sensual experience. I could *feel* as well as hear certain chords on the organ. They passed right through me, as if my body had no substance and no limits, giving rise to a kind of ecstasy I had never known when making love. At the same time, sex with someone I loved took on a kind of purity or holiness, a feeling of union on another level.

This caused me to re-evaluate all of my earlier ideas about religion. Just what is holy anyway? Is a sermon holy if it bores you or leaves you feeling guilty, depressed or smug? Isn't a Monet landscape holy if it makes you aware that we stumble blindfolded through God's miraculous creations? Is a religious denomination holy if it touts the superiority of believers, rather than the unity of all? Can't a performance of *Der Rosenkavalier* or a Mahler symphony be holy if it unites orchestra, singers, and audience, raising them above the petty concerns of the day and making them all feel larger than life?

While organ music and the beauty of the traditional Episcopal service gave me glimpses of another plane of existence, serving as a vestryman did not. When I was asked to join the vestry, I really had no idea what being a vestryman involved, other than passing out programs and ushering people to their seats. I had assumed that vestry meetings focused on the spiritual needs of parishioners, but I soon discovered that the central topics were investments, insurance policies, striking cemetery workers and the conversion of church-owned apartment buildings to other more profitable uses. "Vested interest man" would have been more to the point.

## From Crushing Guilt to Total Joy

About eighteen months after I had returned to the Church, I learned that it is possible to be totally in love with *two* people at the same time. Although this was exhilarating in some ways, it was so contrary to accepted ideas about the nature of love that it triggered overwhelming guilt.

One morning, at about four a.m., I awoke, experiencing this guilt as an almost intolerable weight on my chest, a weight that crushed the breath out of me. In a flash I recalled every shabby or unworthy thing I had ever done, and saw myself as the lowest and most sinful of all people, unfit to live in human society and unworthy of redemption. Then, in the next instant, the room was filled with an indescribable presence, a sensation of light, warmth, music, and total freedom. I _knew_ that I had been forgiven for every wrong I had ever done and that I would die in a state of grace. I went into the living room and sat up until daybreak, crying for joy.

For several days after that, I seemed to be living on another plane. Through some unexplainable shift in my perceptions, the whole world was transformed. Everyone on the streets of Manhattan looked beautiful to me: man or woman, young or old, black or white, rich or poor, bleary-eyed unshaven winos, pathetic bag ladies in shapeless stockings, pompous executives in hand-tailored suits, and stylish matrons who had put in so much resort time that their skin had the look of expensive leather. The rare exceptions were people whose beauty was obscured by a mask of fear or guilt, which sometimes took the outward form of hatred. Even to this day, the awareness that everyone I see is beautiful occasionally takes hold of me, when I am not preoccupied with other matters.

Feeling free from guilt and seeing everyone as beautiful was a joyful experience, but I was troubled by the nagging suspicion that I might be losing my mind. As a native of the Southern Bible Belt, I was all too familiar with accounts of being born again, and therefore skeptical of this religious phenomenon.

Personally, I had always believed that the hallmarks of a truly religious person were ethical behavior, acts of charity, and the quiet, day-to-day application of Christian principles. The thought that the Holy Spirit might be a practical joker who grabs you by the throat, turns your world upside down, and leaves you feeling as limp as overcooked spaghetti, was slightly repugnant to me.

Because of my doubts about my own sanity, I confided in a close friend, Bill Thetford, who happened to be a clinical psychologist. Bill assured me that I was not losing my mind, and even suggested that I was beginning to establish contact with a reality of a different order.

He said that the kind of mystical experience I had described was much more common than most people realized. Bill also admitted that in recent years he himself had become deeply interested in parapsychology and writings on mysticism. Until that time I had supposed that his professional concerns were limited to the traditional subject matter of psychology.

It was comforting to know that Bill did not consider me a likely candidate for a mental institution, but I was a little put out at learning that the remarkable things that had happened to me were "common."

In 1972, when I was planning a European vacation, Bill suggested that I see an English psychic he had found remarkably accurate. Soon after I arrived in London I called for an appointment. When I got to her apartment, the living room was dimly lit and the blinds were drawn against the mid-afternoon sun, for she read auras. She looked nothing like any of the psychics I had ever seen in Hollywood films. Far from being sinister, she was a cheerful middle-class English housewife with a grandmotherly way about her. She asked me to sit in an easy chair in the corner of the room and look directly at her.

Although several people had told me of remarkable "hits" that she had made in her readings for them, I was skeptical of the proceedings and secretly regarded this as nonsense on a cosmic scale.

## "YOU KNEW JESUS"

The psychic seemed to have difficulty reading me, but gave an accurate description of several features of my apartment in New York. Toward the end of the reading, she said, "You and I have very old souls. You knew Jesus."

Later, in the spring of 1979, after the final draft of Andrew's story had been completed, Bill Thetford showed me some notes he had made immediately after seeing this psychic in 1968, four years before I saw her. According to the notes, Bill had asked whether she could give him any information about a close friend with the same given name as myself—let's call him Charles Parsons. She replied: "I don't recognize 'Parsons', but Charles is a writer. He is writing a book concerned with spiritual or psychic matters."

In the spring of 1973, a homosexual love relationship that I had maintained for some thirteen years came to an end. I moved from the Upper West Side to Chelsea and once again drifted away from regular church attendance. I still considered myself religious, but now I understood that everyone on earth belongs to the same church, whether he knows it or not, so that anyone who calls himself a Christian can accomplish more among "sinners" than among those who tithe and sit in pews.

Preaching and proselytizing are not the answer. Rather, we must serve as living proof that love is stronger than hate or fear. At the same time, we must strive never to use other human beings as "objects," whether for personal or institutional ends. It seemed to me that I had been pushed back into the Church to learn precisely this lesson.

## Haunted by the Forgotten

So far as my personal odyssey was concerned, very little happened over the next few years, except that I was plagued by a persistent feeling that *I had forgotten something very important* and that if I could only remember what this was, my whole life would be better for it.

In late fall of 1972, Bill decided to tell me why he had become interested in parapsychology and mysticism. Although these areas of study were anathema to most of his professional peers, a situation that hit very close to home had impelled him to investigate the further reaches of psychology and religion.

A number of years earlier, he had discovered that Helen Schucman, another psychologist with whom he worked closely, was experiencing profound mystical visions. When Helen started hearing an inner voice, she became so upset that she turned to Bill for advice. Bill suggested that since Helen knew shorthand she ought to take down what the voice was saying.

Helen reluctantly agreed, and the inner voice said, "This is a course in miracles. Please take notes."

The result was that Helen and Bill spent some seven years completing what turned out to be *A Course in Miracles*, a three-part work consisting of a basic text, a workbook of 365 lessons, and a teacher's manual. Whenever Helen had time available, she would listen to the inner voice and take notes. Afterward, she would read them back to Bill, who typed them up. The completed work represented a melding of Eastern and Western religious thought, together with some drastic revisions of basic concepts in the dynamics of modern psychology.

## ANOTHER CLOSET SCRIBE

That same night Bill showed me a part of the *Course in Miracles* text, but when I started reading it I was so overcome with emotion that I had to put it down after finishing only three or four pages. Without stopping to think, I said, "This is the ark of the new covenant, which shall be for all mankind." It happened so unexpectedly that I was surprised to hear myself making this ecclesiastical pronouncement.

What I knew of Helen's character made the story of *A Course in Miracles* far more implausible than anything which had happened to me at that point. Helen was a vivacious lady with two passions: statistics and the works of Gilbert and Sullivan. Though born into a well-to-do Jewish family, she was a confirmed atheist and profoundly anti-mystical. In fact, she was so embarrassed by her connection with the *Course* that Bill often characterized her as a "closet scribe."

*A Course in Miracles* was published in 1976. Although I have had a copy in my possession ever since then, I have not yet read it because of a strong conviction that *I was not supposed to do so until something else had been accomplished.*

That "something else" is the book you are now holding.

Not long after Bill first told me about the *Course*, he introduced me to another of his psychologist colleagues, Kenneth Wapnick, a Jew who had become a lay monk in the Roman Catholic Church through a mystical conversion. He was not ordinarily psychic, but when he met me, he immediately saw the name "Andrew" flash across my forehead. He said nothing about this to me at the time, but Bill told me about it the following day.

Then, in the spring of 1977, I began having strange dreams that were unlike any of my earlier dreams. In the first of these, a father and son living on a mountain had struck the rock and tapped a stream of absolute purity, but other men had settled downstream and polluted the water so that it became undrinkable. My understanding of this dream was that the pure mountain stream was the "living water" of the Gospels. The men who had settled downstream were scholars who had revised or reinterpreted the Gospels for unchristian ends, corrupting them and twisting their intended meaning.

In still another dream, I was standing on a dirt footpath, talking with several other gay men, a short distance from the top of a low rise. We were all wearing long tunics made of a rough, unbleached fabric. Something caused us to look to the right, toward the top of the rise. While we were looking in this direction, Jesus materialized there, looking much as he does in classical paintings. He gestured with his left hand, and a large, fierce-looking dog appeared beside him. I heard him call her "Griselda."

## "Don't Panic," Says Jesus

The dog ran down toward us, looking as if she would attack, and stopped beside me. I called her by name and she wagged her tail, obviously wanting to be petted. In the meantime, Jesus also walked down toward us. He saw that we were uneasy and said, "Don't panic. Everything's going to be all right."

Then Jesus motioned to me, indicating that I should leave my friends and walk with him along another path leading off to the right. While we were walking together, I asked, "Isn't it awfully difficult to go through all eternity being perfect?"

"No," he answered, "it's the simplest thing in the world."

The next morning, I looked up "Griselda" in the unabridged dictionary, which noted that this was "…the name of many heroines of Medieval romances, symbolic of humility and long-suffering patience."

My uncertainty about these strange dreams, my peculiar psychic experiences, the odd coincidences in my life, as well as Ken's psychic reference to Andrew, prompted me to try hypnosis, to see whether this might resolve my doubts one way or the other. When I asked Bill's advice about this, he suggested that I see a young *Course in Miracles* teacher named Bruce Gregory, who lived on the West Side of Manhattan. Bruce had worked with a good number of people, using hypnosis for the purpose of recovering past-life memories, sessions that had proven helpful in freeing them from personal blockages and awakening a deeper spiritual awareness.

Bruce was a boyish-looking man in his early thirties, tall, thin and attractive, with a small patch of premature gray in his hair. He was gentle, soft-spoken and enthusiastic and, like myself, a Southerner. Before the session, Bruce explained that the hypnotic approach he would use was basically a relaxation technique, and that I would be conscious the whole time.

## Twenty-five Steps to Another Life

Once I had completely relaxed, we talked for a while about my earliest childhood memories. Then Bruce told me to picture myself at the top of a flight of twenty-five stone steps leading down into an enormous cavern. At the foot of the steps was a door that could be opened by simply lifting the latch. As he counted backwards from twenty-five to one, I was to imagine walking down the steps, one at a time. When I had reached the bottom, he told me to open the door, and said, "Now look around you and tell me what you see."

Before this session I was very dubious about the concept of reincarnation, but had assumed that if any memories of "past lives" emerged from hypnosis, they would involve Jesus or the apostle Andrew. Much to my surprise, I was soon describing myself as wearing "a kind of Brueghel costume" and slipping into the identity of a medieval peasant who was overcome with grief at the death of his young wife. Then I talked about my passing from this existence into the sensation of an afterlife, which was "light and release and freedom."

When Bruce asked me to move into the next "soul experience," I resisted, complaining that I somehow knew it involved *"a test of human endurance—a conflict between body and spirit and a feeling of being torn apart."* Perhaps the story of what happened next can best be told through verbatim excerpts transcribed from the tape recording of the session:

## EXCERPTS FROM THE REGRESSION

**BG:** What is it that is now happening to you?

**CL:** It's...it's the crucifixion. It's Golgotha, and the noise and the people there. How they could be so stupid and cruel? I can't imagine. I've fallen on the ground because I can't look anymore. I don't want to look.

**BG:** What thoughts are going through your mind?

**CL:** The thought that I know that he isn't really dead. But that doesn't seem to matter, the fact that he isn't dead. The horror of that moment is so intense, because they would have killed him if they could. They certainly intended to. It's not so much his suffering as the idea that people could do this, and that they couldn't see what they are doing to themselves.

**BG:** What is happening now?

**CL:** Well, now…now, it's past. We…we've heard that the tomb is open. We can hardly believe it, although we certainly should. There's great…great joy…and great…great fear at the same time, because he won't be there, and we are the ones who have to carry on afterwards. Although we know that he will always be with us in spirit, it's so much more difficult, because we are not really rabbis. How can we know what we should say and do?

(At this point I sat up.)

I'm sorry…I can't…I feel wide awake again.

**BG:** What do you feel now?

**CL:** Just a very confused feeling—a feeling of great joy, along with terrible confusion and fear and lack of confidence.

**BG:** Did you feel that you were alone in that feeling?

**CL:** Oh, no. No, I think we all felt that way.

**BG:** What comes to mind about that?

**CL:** My state of concentration is gone now. I can't see any more….Now that I'm in this state, I don't know what level of reality or fantasy this is….You don't know what the mind has experienced and what it has merely invented.

**BG:** What feeling do you have about this life?

**CL:** A deep sense of personal failure. A feeling that most churches today don't have anything to do with Christianity, and that things aren't the way they were intended to be at all.

**BG:** What is your sense of what was intended?

**CL:** Well, certainly no denominations. The basis was the brotherhood of all men, not the kind of situation we have today, where church is a kind of club membership....They've substituted baptismal rites and confirmation for circumcision. Some people belong, and others don't.

## A DAY OF SHOCK AND DISBELIEF

The night of this first hypnotic session, I was besieged by so many thoughts, images, doubts and conflicting emotions that I hardly slept at all. The next day I felt drained and exhausted.

This venture into hypnosis was very different from what I had imagined it would be. I had supposed that I would be in an almost trancelike state, so that I would not know what had gone on until I played back the tape. Instead, I was fully conscious the whole time and could hardly believe the things I was saying. As a red-blooded, 100% gay American, I was shocked by the images of an earlier life in which my consuming passion had been the love of one woman. Until this time I had never had any dream or fantasy resembling this.

Also, I had regarded hypnosis as an intellectual exercise, assuming that I would gain information from it by reading it as I might read a scholarly essay or the report of a psychological experiment. For this reason the emotionality of the experience— the long pauses, the heavy breathing, the sobs—stunned me.

Along with this, I began to have a sense of wholeness that I had never known before, for it seemed that I wasn't really very different from heterosexuals after all. It now seemed that my previous conception of myself had been very one-dimensional and incomplete, like the flat world of the pre-Columbian period.

Originally, I had intended to arrange for a second hypnotic session the following week, but the intensity of the first session was so great that I had to allow myself more time to integrate it. After four weeks, I still had many questions and decided to try again.

The second session seemed very inconclusive to me, although Bruce felt that I had produced some worthwhile material. Somehow I couldn't quite block out my awareness that it was 1977, and that I was in a studio apartment on the Upper West Side of Manhattan.

## "IF IT IS TO BE..."

Two days after the second session, as I went for a walk on my lunch hour, I said to myself, and yet not to myself, *"If it is to be, let it be."*

That same evening a rushing flood of impressions began to crowd out my conscious thoughts, and I experienced all of these as memories, rather than the creation of my own mind. Words started forming in my head, and certain images. Every morning I began waking up at three-thirty or four a.m. and writing these down. By the following weekend I had typed up nearly fifty pages of Andrew's story. I had also lost more than five pounds, even though I wasn't overweight to begin with.

The words of Jesus were clearer to me than anything else. I could set these down exactly as they came to me. The visual images were harder, because I had to attempt to describe these in my own words. The names of people and places were most difficult of all.

During this time I consulted a few references. I knew that the story forming in my mind identified me with an apostle, but I didn't know which apostle I was. However, I did know that there was intense conflict between myself and my brother, also an apostle, and that I had a lover who was still another member of the twelve.

Starting with the fact that my friend's colleague, Ken Wapnick, had associated me with Andrew, and with my personal knowledge that Andrew was the brother of Simon Peter, I devoted most of my limited research to Andrew. I read *The Acts of Andrew* (ca.150-200 C.E.) and found that it deserved to be in the New Testament Apocrypha, being full of camels walking through the eyes of needles and other phony miracles.

One source told me that Andrew and his brother Simon came from the town of Bethsaida, in Galilee, and that Philip came from this same town. Another Biblical scholar described Philip and Andrew as "virtually inseparable." When this was pieced together with some of the images I had seen, the relationship between Philip and Andrew was clear to me.

When I first started working on this book, I would walk about the streets of midtown Manhattan on my lunch hour, seeing images of myself in the workingman's tunic of Biblical times. My image of Andrew didn't match the face and body I see in the bathroom mirror when I shave. He was about the same height, but squarer and somewhat heavier, with darker eyes and auburn hair. Nevertheless, I knew that we shared a common identity. His thoughts ran through my mind. I experienced his guilt, his love, his joy and his suffering as my own.

In a scene that I saw vividly many times, Andrew was standing—no, *I was standing*—near a grove of small trees on the shore of a lake that stretched as far as the eye could see, watching a beautiful young man bathing himself. At other times I would see myself lying unconscious within sight of the cross.

Finally, I saw myself stripped naked and head down, nailed to an X-shaped cross, and hoped the passers-by on 47th Street wouldn't notice the tears welling in my eyes.

New York, New York
November 20, 1980

# AFTERWORD TO THE BOOK OF ANDREW

By Charles C. Lehman

W hile you have just finished reading about Andrew's life, I have actually experienced its events as happening to me. At this point, that initial shock of feeling myself in another time and place, in another man's skin, has long since passed, but the implications of Andrew's story continue to percolate through my consciousness, forcing me to re-examine my personal goals and rethink my earlier assumptions about the nature of life. Since these implications may not be entirely clear from the text itself, I want to make them explicit.

**First off, this book stands any dogmatic or denomi-national conception of Christianity on its head.** According to *The Book of Andrew*, no existing church or combination of churches truly embodies the teachings of Jesus. In fact, the kind of religion described here cannot be institutionalized, because worship cannot be confined to a particular setting or a given day of the week. Any attempt to standardize religious experience cuts us off from our primary sources of enlightenment. The increase in understanding that we must ultimately achieve can come about only in direct person-to-person or God-to-person encounters.

**The Jesus presented here does not say that acceptance of his Godhood is indispensable to salvation, neither does he describe his crucifixion as a symbolic sacrifice for all mankind.** Salvation is open to everyone, regardless of our formal religious creed. It comes about through a pervasive, joyful love for God and all His creations, through personal actions in keeping with that love, and by a continuous increase in our understanding of our proper relationship to God and others, leading to ultimate spiritual unity.

**Second, instead of being condemned to eternal damnation, all of us will ultimately attain the Kingdom of God, whether we are consciously seeking it in this particular lifetime or not.** There is no Hell, save for that hell which we ourselves have created here on earth.

**The concept of sin is drastically transformed.** Sin is not the creation of an inherently evil spirit; it is the consequence of limited understanding and insecurity stemming from feelings of separation from God. What we call sin is always subject to correction and *will be corrected* in time.

**Things that the established Church has defined as "mortal" sins may not be sinful at all.** "Unnatural" sexual acts between two men or two women can be holy if they spring from a mutual desire for spiritual union. These acts are less exalted than the spiritual love of God and all people everywhere, but no less exalted than "natural" heterosexual acts.

**In contrast, human greed, which the world usually justifies on the grounds that one must "provide for" one's family, is treated as a serious deficiency in understanding.**

The established Church has glossed over Jesus's warnings against greed, because some of the greediest among us have tried to exorcise their guilt feelings or achieve higher status by becoming the greatest benefactors of the Church.

## THIS VERY MOMENT IS ETERNITY

**Above all else, love is clearly the central focus of *The Book of Andrew*.** All work, all worship, all life is distilled into this supreme concept. If we open ourselves fully to the experience of love, we cannot sin, because we enter directly into the Kingdom of God.

If this strikes you as a very simple-minded approach to religion, then I must confess that the simple brand of religion presented in these pages is much more congenial to me than the creed of any denomination I can think of.

If there seem to be curious gaps in Andrew's story, it is because I have set down only those things that came to me in the manner described in "A Personal History." It didn't seem right to piece out the narrative by borrowing or paraphrasing other elements in the familiar Bible story. Therefore, you will find no immaculate conception, no virgin birth, no walking on water, no miracle of the loaves and fishes, no temptation on the mountain top, no last supper, and so on.

Although the places and events described in Andrew's story were vivid and immediate when I set them down, they seem very distant now. This is as it should be. There is no point in endlessly reliving past lives in order to escape present responsibilities. Neither is there any point in using the memories of reincarnation to achieve the dubious status that one has missed in this life. Images of past lives have value only if they can serve as guideposts in our lives today. After all, what we are properly concerned with is the here and now.

This very moment is eternity.

## SHARING A NEVER-ENDING BOUNTY

How can the simple message in this book apply to our complex human problems in today's world? I say it can apply directly. On the most fundamental human level we haven't changed that much in the last two thousand years, although our mushrooming technology may give rise to the illusion of human change.

Human uncertainty about our ultimate fate is still a major source of confusion and anxiety. Do we have a few brief years of life followed by nothingness, or do we have a grip on eternity? If we are limited to a single life, then we may feel justified in behaving like children who expect to have only one crack at the candy store, grabbing every chocolate bar within reach and screaming in rage at any other child who threatens to deprive us of the smallest jellybean. But if we all share a never-ending bounty, such childish greed is worse than pointless.

The trick is to keep our faith that the "candy store" will always be open, even when all the other kids are scratching, kicking, grabbing and yelling, "Mine! Mine!"

Mankind is frequently defined as a social animal, but I would go further than that: I believe that each of us has a built-in unconscious knowledge that we are all one, even though we limit our spiritual awareness by pinning on meaningless labels like "Jew," "Arab," "liberal," "conservative," "straight," or "gay."

Indeed, I believe that the unconscious force within us, pushing us toward unity with all other people, is the voice of the Holy Spirit. Whenever we ignore this voice or try to thwart it, we are breaking the highest Law of all.

## FORGIVENESS, BRIDGE TO UNITY

Why must we continually defend ourselves against this happiest and most basic of all truths? Coming to *experience* the single universal unity of all men and women is the only real hope for individual fulfillment and for the salvation of our world, yet we continue to behave as if it were the greatest threat to our existence.

If, as I believe, there is something of God in each of us, then we can never experience the indescribable joy of God within ourselves, so long as we persist in our ego's denial of our unity with all other people, because this amounts to shutting out a part of God's reality. If we honestly start to examine the economic, social, and intellectual devices our egos use to erect barriers between ourselves and others, we will come to discover why all of us who had been seeking happiness and security, with the ego as our guide, have ended up feeling guilty, lonely, empty, bitter, and dead.

It is not enough to say that we are all one: we must act on the basis of that unity. But this is such a radical departure from our customary way of doing things that many of us may not be able to achieve it by a simple about-face. We are not talking about toying with a new intellectual concept. If we take the time to reread *The Book of Andrew*, we will discover Jesus's teachings on forgiveness and universal love as central to everything he came to share. We will find that forgiveness is an active process undertaken, with the Holy Spirit's help, to cleanse the way we have perceived both ourselves and others, so that we then discover a new reality that is of God, a reality that can only be responded to by unconditional love.

The forgiveness Jesus came to teach is the bridge we all need to cross to discover the love, unity, and oneness we all share in God.

If we presently find it difficult to forgive by opening ourselves to the Holy Spirit, we can start to discover what might be called the "flip side" of unity with others. What we now perceive in others actually says a lot about our own beliefs about ourselves. If we take anyone outside of ourselves and seek to identify with them, looking for what we like and dislike in them, we will start to discover ways in which we are very similar. Psychologists call this "projection," and our own recognition of this can be quite startling.

## "I Am That One"

We might begin by saying to ourselves: I am that mother of four small children, living on welfare. I am that neo-Nazi consumed by hatred beyond his understanding. I am that elderly widow in a nursing home, abandoned by her family. I am that suburban teenager overwhelmed by boredom, his own sexuality and a life without purpose. I am that aging chairman of the board, hard pushed by younger executives and hated by his own family. I am that prostitute, used by her customers, harassed by the police and beaten up by her pimp.

This is only the tip of the iceberg, for the varieties of human misery are endless. But if we can really apply ourselves to this exercise in imagination, if we can *feel* what it is like to be all kinds of people, we will find that we are much closer to these seemingly "different" people than we first thought, sharing the same *content* of thoughts and feelings, although the *forms* the people take may differ from our own. And by seeking to experience what it must be like to "be in their skin," or "walk in their moccasins for a moon," we may in fact discover a new compassion awakening in us.

There is a pointed irony in calling this an exercise in imagination. In fact, all forms of human misery (including yours and mine) are not real, according to Jesus, but fantasies, born out of guilt and nurtured by separation. Loneliness and despair are phantoms haunting the dark night of the soul. Under the blazing sun of love they melt away.

## AN END TO RECYCLING HATREDS

Having seen the failure of all earlier efforts at wholeness and peace of mind, each generation is desperately seeking alternatives. While their search may sometimes be lost in empty pleasures, experimentation with drugs, or mindless cruelty, I believe that the present age is a transitional period that may ultimately lead to a new social order greater than any our world has ever known before.

Why should we go on reliving the hatreds and hang-ups of our parents, grandparents and great-grandparents? Hasn't our age-old worldwide guilt trip gone on long enough? Let's put an end to it and get on with the loving! (Or let's start with the loving and our guilt trip will automatically come to an end.)

In the seemingly unlikely event that we could achieve a world in which guilt is entirely displaced by love, what would we have? Would we be stuck with a sugar-coated, pole-to-pole Disneyland populated entirely by lotus eaters? Would all intellectual progress, all scientific advancement and all artistic innovation cease? Would succeeding generations revolt against the stifling banality of this new order? I cannot believe that any of these things would happen, although there would certainly be a drastic reordering of our priorities and activities.

As God has given us our spirits, so He has given us our minds and hands, which are meant to be used in His service. If love is one face of joy, then work is the other. We must not allow our intellectual abilities or our manual skills to waste away, simply because we have an abiding faith in God's mercy and goodness. We must use all our talents in God's service, whether these talents are spiritual, mental, or physical.

## A LONELY LEGACY

In truth, we have a great deal of work to do. Thousands of years of wrong thinking and separation from God and our fellow man have left us a monstrous legacy of misery, loneliness and despair. We have reached the point where there must be hundreds of millions of people who do not believe in the reality of love. Convincing all those who are naked, starving, or oppressed that love exists will be a superhuman task.

If we expect to make meaningful progress toward a better world, we must realize that we cannot begin by changing "the system." The initial change must come within ourselves, for in fact we are the system. Once the light of love has been turned on within us, it cannot be contained, it cannot be sidetracked, it cannot be put out, for it will grow and grow and grow, until it lights the whole world.

Perhaps I should point out that this book isn't only about love, worship and unity. It also concerns the experience of being gay. What am I trying to tell you about that?

*[Editor's Note: As an editorial aside, I would like to remind the reader that Chuck's Afterword was written in 1980, and this book is being first released in 2013, a 33-year period in which remarkable progress in greater acceptance of gays and lesbians has been achieved, particularly among younger people, the military, and in a larger percentage of the general public. But still there exist pockets of deep rejection that are causing conflict, violence, and even death. So Chuck's comments still have great relevance to the present day.]*

## BE BOTH VULNERABLE AND INVINCIBLE

If you are also gay, then I am telling you that you are just as good as anyone else and not as different as you may suppose. Your ties to the straight community are as important as your personal love life. We are all born into the same total human family. No one can take that birthright from you, and you cannot voluntarily renounce it.

As a homosexual, you are not limited to the two old options of: (A) living your entire life in the closet, or (B) withdrawing to a gay ghetto. Along with your obligation to join in the mainstream of human concerns, you have the right to be yourself wherever you are. You can love everyone every day of your life. You can be totally vulnerable and completely invincible at the same time. Start now!

If you are straight, I am giving you the same basic message: gay people are an integral part of your life. In order to reach the fullest, most joyful expression of your own sexuality, you must recognize that other ways of love exist and that these are equally miraculous. Unless you do this, you are merely acting out the stereotyped role of "a man" or "a woman," even in your most intimate moments. As long as you limit yourself to being a stereotype, you will never appreciate your own uniqueness.

If what I say is true, why should homosexuals make you uncomfortable? I don't know all the possible reasons, but I do know it's time well spent understanding all that we resist, until we can find a way to let a deeper love replace our fears.

## PORK, SHELLFISH, AND SAME-SEX LOVE

If you discover that your religious training has formed your opinions against gays and lesbians, you might dig a little deeper and discover that other condemnations found in the Bible have been purposely ignored as "old fashioned," such as those condemning pork, shellfish, and divorce. Ask yourself what Jesus said about homosexuality and discover he said nothing in the Bible except to love God and your neighbor as yourself.

The fears and anxieties that straight men and women have about homosexuality often seem to focus on their own children. You might have to face a very hard question as to whether you are more concerned about the happiness, well-being, and freedom of your children or your own reputation in the face of raising a child who is "different." You may also have to determine the real truth about a number of commonly accepted beliefs about homosexuality that may be guiding you, by stepping outside your comfort zone and reaching out to those who might counsel and explain and give you the facts.

Even though you are exclusively heterosexual now, you may feel guilty about a past homosexual attachment to a high-school friend. But if it seemed beautiful at the time, why should it cause you pain now? Unless you choose to make it an issue, this has nothing to do with your present realities. Facing it honestly may even make you a better father or mother.

You may believe that you have failed as a parent because you suspect that one of your children has gay tendencies. If this is the case, let me assure you that you have nothing to do with your children's sexual tendencies. Your children will be heterosexual, homosexual, bisexual or asexual because that's what they are. Why not love them as they *are*, rather than trying to force them into emotional straightjackets that don't fit?

## GAY MICHELANGELO OR STRAIGHT STALIN?

Instead of being so concerned about your children's sexual preferences, I would encourage you to prepare them to be courageous, outgoing, and loving. This I believe is your basic responsibility as a mother or father. Would you rather be the parent of a gay Michelangelo or a straight Stalin? Since homosexuals have always been around and appear to be born in fairly steady numbers, why not relax and love us? Given half a chance, we can be very lovable.

Instead of setting up barricades between the straight and gay communities, let us start building bridges. If you are gay, find some loving, non-threatening way of coming out to your family and your most trusted straight friends. Show them that your life is as happy as theirs, that being gay is not a character fault or a sickness, but an alternate expression of human love.

If you are straight, the lives of gay people already touch your life—unless you are a hermit. You probably already know which of your friends, relatives, or children are gay. Let them know that you love them, not out of phony piety or compassion, but because all of us are special, whether we are straight or gay.

It took me a long time to decide that I should try to find a publisher for this book. It took even longer to reconcile myself to the idea of publishing it under my own name, since this may destroy the rather comfortable anonymity I have become accustomed to over the years. Now I have no idea what will happen to my life, either personally or professionally, but perhaps this is what a leap of faith is all about.

In the end, publishing the book anonymously or under a pen name seemed contrary to the whole spirit of the work and an unthinkable act of cowardice, as well. If Andrew and Philip are to come out of their closets after all these years, it is only fair that I should also. Perhaps we are approaching that time when "all hearts shall be opened and everything which is in the soul of man made known."

All I know is that I have never been happier than I am at this moment, because now I can be fully conscious, fully human and totally myself. I cannot arrive at a precise definition of this work, but it is somehow bound up with the whole purpose of my life. Whatever the future holds, I rush into it headlong and without regret.

Our only two sources of information about God or the nature of the spiritual universe are first-hand experience and the oral or written reports of others. Perhaps many of us are incapable of that powerful, wordless awareness of the presence of the Holy Spirit until the words of others have alerted us to the possibility that it *can* happen.

Sometimes I talk about this book as a genuine revelation, don't I? Well, so it has been for me, since I have found great joy as well as great pain in the writing of it. It has given me a greater sense of personal integrity and courage than I have ever had before.

Since you have stayed with me this far, I should like to ask one last favor of you. Regardless of your religious convictions, your sexual proclivities, or your opinion of this book, please give at least passing consideration to three simple ideas given to us by a man from Nazareth who walked the earth a long time ago. You can find the same three statements in the works of Matthew, Mark, Luke, and John, but only if you read between the lines:

*Love is worship.*
*Life is joy.*
*God is in all of us.*

New York, New York
1980

From the Editor of *The Book of Andrew*:

# A Touching Fragment from the Life of Jesus

## and Lessons from Charles Lehman's Last Regression

By Bruce M. Gregory

W ell, what do *you* make of it all, dear reader? *You're* the important one now.

I've lived with the revelations in this book since 1977, and think of it as a restored gospel and "Holy Writ." It's as if we've unexpectedly discovered a portrait, a powerful masterpiece, underneath the lesser, painted-over version that had been produced by the artist's studio assistants. First the disbelief, then the awe.

I'll be honest. Both Charles and I never felt disbelief about Andrew. You see, both of us had our own separate clues while growing up that made it easier to later accept the reality and the power of *The Book of Andrew*.

## "My Name Is *Andrew*," Said Little Charles

In 2007, Charles's older surviving sister shared with me two early memories that caught my attention. As a youngster, he had complained about being named Charles and said he wished he had been named *Andrew*. And many years ago his mother told

Charles and his two sisters that she had dreamed Charles had written a book titled *The Golden Citadel*. Charles wrote only one book, *The Book of Andrew.*

Now, a citadel is defined as a medieval fortress of protection for a town, positioned as the last line of defense. A "golden" citadel has never existed physically, but as a symbol it could stand for the last line of defense of Truth, which is a powerful way of defining *The Book of Andrew.*

And you might remember reading the following two significant passages in Charles's 1980 "A Personal History," found earlier in Part II:

"So far as my personal odyssey was concerned, very little happened over the next few years, except that I was plagued by a persistent feeling that I had forgotten something very important and that if I could only remember what this was, my whole life would be better for it."

And also this excerpt, "*A Course in Miracles* was published in 1976. Although I have had a copy in my possession ever since then, I have not yet read it because of a strong conviction that I was not supposed to do so until something else had been accomplished. That 'something else' is *the book you are now holding.*"

Charles somehow knew, more than a full year before *Andrew* even got started, that he had forgotten something critically important and was not to read the inspired words of Jesus in the modern *A Course in Miracles*, for another unknown reason, which he dutifully obeyed. *A Course in Miracles* and *The Book of Andrew* were received separately, but if you read them both, you will hear the same voice and the same mind animating each page. This consistency is even more remarkable when you consider that Charles followed his guidance to postpone reading the *Course* until *Andrew* was completed.

What about our joint connection? In a letter to me in1977, Chuck wrote, "If this should ever be published, this means that anyone who reads *The Book of Andrew* and knows you well will probably be able to identify your role in it. Naturally, if you prefer, I will change your initials and make your description less specific. *However, my present intuition is that we will one day be involved in a joint enterprise, so we may be identified with one another anyway.* Peace, Chuck."

We remained in close touch and collaboration from 1977 until 1999, when he died.

## A Prophetic Message From an Angel

Was there any clue in my own life that might have indicated such an extraordinary joint enterprise as publishing a restored gospel with the authentic voice of Jesus?

Yes. For one thing, all my life I've felt a real dissatisfaction with the way Jesus has been portrayed in the New Testament— partly loving and partly vindictive. I felt something was definitely wrong. I kept looking, year after year, unsuccessfully, for the real Jesus, until I found him, first in *A Course in Miracles* and then, a year later, in the beginnings of *The Book of Andrew*.

Oh, and then there was my early message from an angel. I started out this life a bit shy and fearful of others, though I was born into a loving family with deep spiritual roots. Between the ages of three and four, I had an encounter in the woods with what I somehow knew to be an angel, who spoke to me mind-to-mind about how important it was to remember that I had agreed to help with something important in this life. I remember closing my eyes and repeating, *"I must remember. I must remember. I must remember."*

The angel was gone when I opened my eyes. I told no one about this for many years, but the memory of the encounter was always there on a back burner, as I wondered which of my life's turns might be the one.

Now I know. *This is it.*

I see *The Book of Andrew* as being on the same ultimate level of inspiration as the revered *A Course in Miracles* (www.acim.org), which also appeared in print in the 1970s from an inspired source and went on to worldwide acclaim. There have been over two million copies of the *Course* sold in English so far, as well as publication in twenty languages, with three more in the works, all without a single word of advertising. Truth is its own best messenger.

These two life-changing texts complement each other. To me, *The Book of Andrew* is the original version of Jesus's teachings and *A Course in Miracles*, which is a powerful training in awakening the Spirit, is Jesus's latter-day correction of New Testament teachings.

## A Letter from Chuck Lehman, 1988

To take you a bit behind the scenes, to get more of a sense of Charles's perspective, you might enjoy reading a semi-playful letter he sent me in 1988.

*April 24, 1988*

*Dear Bruce,*

*Is it starting all over again? I thought that kind of thing was behind me, but I got up at 3:55 a.m. Saturday morning to jot down the fragment below. I can't vouch for its quality, but it does seem to shed some light on the passage, "Suffer little children to come unto me..."*

*Certainly I would like to feel that my book is complete and that the many rough edges have been smoothed out, but you know as well as I that the job of doing that would be a pain in the ass. I'll be exhausted! And when would I be able to read the Sunday* New York Times? *The only good thing you can say for it is that it's one way to lose weight.*

*I hadn't looked at the book in a long time and wanted to make sure that I still had a copy of the complete manuscript. That's how I happened to reread the first two chapters just now. Somewhat to my surprise, I discovered that, for all its faults, it is a fairly powerful work. In my mind, I usually think of it as being cornier and more awkwardly expressed than it is in fact.*

*So what else can I tell you? Next time around, I want some function other than gay scribe.*

*Love, Chuck*

Below is the touching view of Jesus, received by Charles in 1988, that he referred to in the letter above.

*The infant boy standing in the lap of Jesus looked up at him and tugged at his beard. Jesus laughed heartily and held the child up at arm's length.*

*"Well, what is this? Would you unwhisker a learned rabbi and prophet? Take care lest you be carried away in a great chariot borne by the west wind, or struck by a thunderbolt."*

*Jesus clutched the boy to himself. The infant buried his face in the folds of Jesus's garment and laughed, as if he had understood what Jesus had said so playfully.*

*"What wonders of creation children are! Lacking the heavy words that weigh down the spirit, the tearful memories of yesterday or the fears of tomorrow, they live in the eternal Kingdom of God— until we have taught them not to do so.*

*"If you too would know the Kingdom of God, my dear followers and friends, become like this child. Forget all else, that you might recall the infinite goodness of Him Who is the Father of us all."*

*Then Jesus handed the infant back to his joyful mother and stooped to hear what a small girl would whisper in his ear.*

This lovely last fragment never found its spot in the text of *The Book of Andrew*, but it gives you an example of how each nightly transmission given to Charles was shaped into a whole for insertion into an eventual text.

Perhaps, if the text of *The Book of Andrew* had been found in an ancient jar near an archeological site, some scholars might consider it a worthy contribution to the field of New Testament studies. But it wasn't. It came in a series of inspired revelations, spurred on by two past-life regressions I guided, a modality that, thankfully, is being taken much more seriously as a therapeutic practice these days.

And finally, one more inspired transmission. This one emerged from a dream that Charles Lehman had one month after his dear friend Bill Thetford passed away on July 4, 1988. Chuck felt it must have come from Bill who, with Helen Schucman, received *A Course in Miracles* and brought it into the world. If you will, let yourself enjoy this meditation on a daily basis, perhaps starting your day with it, or ending the night on this gentle note.

You may very well find yourself having your own mystical experiences.

## CHARLES'S DREAM MEDITATION

*After familiarizing yourself with these instructions, close your eyes. Know your Self as the core of a sphere radiating infinitely far in all directions—above your head, beneath your feet, before you and behind you, to your left and to your right. Feel that eternal, never-failing truth. Now it is clear that the shell of illusion, comprising the body and the proximate senses of sight, hearing, touch, taste and smell, is but a minuscule fraction of your total reality, hardly worthy of notice. Neither pain nor pleasure can intrude upon the stillness of your being.*

*You can never be imprisoned by time or space. Nor can you ever be separated from the Soul of God, or from the Souls of your brothers and sisters, present, departed, or yet unborn.*

## CHARLES LEHMAN'S REVEALING LAST REGRESSION

In 1995, four years before Charles's death, I was back in New

York, doing some regressions, and Charles asked if we might do one more session. It had been eighteen years since the last one, and he felt something was incomplete. It wasn't about *The Book of Andrew*. He needed to understand something deep and unresolved in his own soul.

We used the same approach—deep relaxation and guided meditation. His first early memory from his present life concerned being so much younger than everyone else in his family and having no say-so during the time of his mother and father's separation over issues of quarreling and intimacy. Even though he also remembered having a Christmas tree with real candles, it was not a picture of a perfect childhood.

When asked to create his ideal retreat while in trance, Charles went directly to a past life as a monk in a Franciscan monastery cell in medieval southern France. He had left behind an outside life that had been far from serene, finding a wonderful sense of peace in this very simple setting. By doing what his inner guidance indicated was the will of God, he would find tranquility, even if ninety-nine out of a hundred others suggested something else. This critical theme of peace would come up again and tie the loose ends together.

When asked to remember another past life, he found himself in Paris during the 1500s, in a lively scene with a lot of people. He described himself as a craftsman, a shoemaker, recently married to a woman with a very cheerful face. When I asked him to move forward to the next most important event in this life, he became frantic over the disappearance of his very beautiful wife, feeling she had been abducted by someone of the powerful, corrupt nobility, and knowing he would never again see her alive. As in that first regression, he was devastated that his wife was gone, but this time he was able to take comfort in the idea that they had loved each other so much since childhood that she would never leave him of her own free will.

He then spoke, more from his soul's perspective, knowing that the two of them would meet again in another lifetime, in another identity, perhaps even another sexual orientation. It gave him some degree of peace in that life to decide not to remarry, to continue to do his menial but necessary work as a cobbler, and to find comfort in the familiar rituals of his local parish church, St. Julien-le-Pauvre, on the Left Bank.

## SUFFERING THE LOSS OF SIMON AGAIN

I asked him to move to another past life and, instead of another unknown one, Charles returned to the time of Andrew and Philip, picking up the theme of the painful loss of loved ones— losing Philip, losing Jesus, and losing the love of his elder brother, Simon, whom we know as Peter. As Andrew, he couldn't accept any of this suffering, particularly the crucifixion of Jesus, as being the will of God. To him it was the mistake of men, the worst mistake ever made in the world. And he felt the tragic price he had to pay for loving Philip: the loss of his brother Simon's love, to the point of Simon's disowning him. Charles yearned with the hope that one day Simon would come to love him again.

Charles continued exploring that biblical life, remembering the idyllic childhood he shared with Philip, even before their mature love for each other awakened. He was then confronted with the later painful memory of being asked by Jesus to separate from Philip in order to take the missionary work on separate roads. The wrenching contrast between enjoying idyllic love and then being apart from that love, knowing most probably that Philip was soon to be crucified, awakened a sublime realization in present-day Charles.

He said to me: "I guess eventually what that really means is that there is life beyond life and that we never really lose anyone who is dear to us; and we never even know how many people are dear to us. There are so many, such a vast crowd, and the people who have been important to me in this life are people...all people I've known before." Here he was restating the lofty belief he took from the cobbler's life, that we never really lose anyone we love, but adding a new and powerful insight: the concept of the *group reincarnation of souls* we have known and loved from other lives.

## A Saintly Abbot Appears Centuries Later

Drawing on this new theme, Charles, still in trance, brought to mind a remarkable present-day chaplain, an ordained minister who had agreed without any reservation to serve as a spiritual advisor to Charles's gay veteran's group in New York. The chaplain's "Well, yes, by all means" acceptance and "It's an honor to be asked" went a long way beyond tolerance or acceptance. It revealed a rare kind of love and willingness to be associated with "outcasts," Charles felt, thinking there was really something Christlike about that.

When I asked him to take a glimpse at another past

life, Charles found himself back in the medieval Franciscan monastery, and realized it was there that he had known the saintly chaplain. The chaplain had been Abbot Anselm, head of the monastery, who had not only sought to provide meaningful, pleasurable work for all the monks, but ensured peace by eliminating political struggles and instilling a constant sense of God's presence at all times in his monastery.

With this vision, Charles announced that he had come to the end of the session, as this last discovery had given him the comfort he realized he was seeking.

## "New Friends" Are Old Ones We Recognize

Charles's death from cancer would take place in a few years. Somehow he knew that he needed this final regression in order to weave together several themes—isolation, suffering, and loss—with his new realizations about love and a timeless perspective. He emerged from the regression with a deep sense of peace and comfort that prepared him for his eventual transition. Though he had experienced some of the most wrenching and devastating losses humans can suffer, he had also experienced the infinite peace of re-entering Heaven after finishing his peasant farmer life, as well as the comforting presence of Philip and Jesus after both their tragic deaths, and at his own death by crucifixion as well. He had seen enough to know that death is an illusion. And he had come to know, through a deep spiritual memory, that we are all surrounded by loved ones who have been close in past lives and have come along with us in this life to nurture, support and encourage us in what you might call a team effort.

In other words, we don't really "make" friends, we recognize them.

Charles also found, in his life as Andrew, under Jesus's guidance, and in his monastery life under the saintly Abbot, that we are surrounded by the very presence of God, if we learn to become aware of it and consciously cultivate it. By his own admission, Charles found his 20th-century life lit by the presence of God as he witnessed the beauty and illumination that was ever-present in the lives of all he saw or met on a daily basis. Charles's life and testimony are strong sources of inspiration for us all in our quest for meaning and peace.

Only by looking deeper than tragedy, as Charles set out to do, can we find the transcendent truth that we are forever surrounded by a love that heals and transforms us.

Remember his words, *"There is life beyond life…We never really lose anyone who is dear to us…and the people important to me in this life are people I've known before."*

## A Brief Study Guide to *The Book of Andrew*

It is important to ask the questions *"Why The Book of Andrew?"* and *"Why now?"*

In Chapter 10, "The Last Teaching," Jesus gives Andrew a commission: "…I charge you to remember everything that has passed between us, for **false doctrines will be spread in my name**, and seeds of judgment, hate and death will be sown by those who call themselves my followers. Also, **I have told you things which are not to be given to the world at this time.** Yet, when the time is ripe, you will open your heart and bear witness, setting down my true sayings that proclaim *God's love for all His children.*"

The text of *Andrew* explains that Simon (Simon Peter) and Paul (Saul of Tarsus) were most responsible, after Jesus's final departure, for his teachings being perverted and false doctrines spread throughout the world, based on their *lack of understanding*, though no condemnation is offered, as "the love of God in all, by all, for all, will still all argument and right all error." Chapter 8, "The Ministry and Teachings of Jesus," and Chapter 10, "The Last Teaching," contain the clearest expositions of Jesus's *undistorted* teachings.

If you simply read these sections carefully, as if Jesus were speaking directly to you, honestly determining where your present approach differs with Jesus, you will see the gaps. One example is the section in Chapter 8 directed to Labbaeus ("Even a child is known by his own doings, whether these be good or evil") on the dedicated use of unconditional love. The biggest challenge to accepting all of Jesus's teachings arises when they run contrary to both our egos and to the ways of the world. It's only in the application, the daily implementation of his teachings, that we discover their validity and power to transform our lives and heal our broken relationships.

## No Hell, but All the Learning Lives We Need

One topic, the issue of having lived past lives, might seem to be one the world wasn't ready for at the time of Jesus's ministry.

Ask most Christians today about reincarnation, and

many will quote "once to live and once to die," a popularization of Hebrews 9:27 ("And just as it is appointed for mortals to die once, and after that the judgment"). But a closer look in the New Testament reveals four passages that reflect an *understanding* of reincarnation: John 9:2 ("His disciples asked him, 'Rabbi, who sinned, this man or his parents, that he was born blind?'"); Mark 8:27 ("Who do people say that I am?"), which the disciples answered with "John the Baptist" (presumably already beheaded), Elijah, or one of the long-gone prophets; Matthew 11:13-15 ("For all the prophets and the law until John [the Baptist] came; and if you are willing to accept it, He is Elijah who is to come, let anyone with ears listen!"); and Matthew 17:10-13 ("And the disciples asked him, 'Why, then, do the scribes say that Elijah must come first?' [before the Messiah] He replied, 'Elijah is indeed coming and will restore all things; but I tell you that Elijah has already come, and they did not recognize him, but they did to him whatever they pleased [decapitated him]. So also the Son of Man is about to suffer at their hands.' Then the disciples understood that he was speaking about John the Baptist.")

With Jesus and his disciples, reincarnation was *neither unknown nor condemned*. That role of condemnation, according to history, is assigned to Emperor Justinian, influenced by his Empress Theodora, who had the Council of Constantinople issue anathema edicts in 553 AD against the beliefs of the beloved earlier theologian, Origen, who promoted the idea that all souls would eventually be saved from their separation from God, through the spiritual awakening that occurs after living many lives. The force of multiple anathema edicts against Origen's teachings was enough to bury reincarnation for most Christians, but it obviously had no effect on the continual reincarnation of souls worldwide. As the old joke goes, *"I don't believe in reincarnation, and I didn't believe the last time either!"*

Look at the section in Chapter 8 of *The Book of Andrew*, where Jesus addresses Simon with the question, "Who do men say that I am?" Jesus makes his teaching on reincarnation very clear to Simon and to all the disciples with the statement, "When I say to all of you that your souls are eternal, I speak not only of Paradise and the life hereafter, but also of *other lives which are long forgotten.*" And toward the end of Chapter 8, in the section on the story of the prodigal son, Jesus states, "No one may master the lessons of Heaven in a single life, but God, a loving Father, does not decree for His children the fire of eternal damnation. Rather, He repeats His lessons with patience beyond the understanding of men, giving His children all the time they need to learn. This is why I say to you, *you must be born again.* Time after time you will be born of the flesh, but when, after many lives, you have learned the lessons of Heaven, you will be born of the Spirit. From that time on, eternal Paradise is yours."

What then is the topic that Jesus felt the world wasn't ready for 2,000 years ago? It turns out to be Jesus's true teachings about *God's love for all His children,* found in Chapter 3: "I tell you this day, Andrew, that you must be born again. You will live many lives, until you have learned all the lessons you must master. You will live both as man and woman. In some lives you will love only women; in other lives, only men, and in others both women and men. This is true for all mortals, even your brother, Simon....In truth, those we call mortals are immortal, from everlasting to everlasting. The body in which you dwell today is but the merest shadow of your eternal soul. *Seeing that in different lives the same soul may love a man or a woman, what can it matter in the eyes of God whether you love a man or woman in this life, if only you love in God's name?"*

## THE SAME-SEX LOVE OF *FOUR* APOSTLES

Those of us who pulled the gay lever before taking a body this time might wonder why such a revelation as Jesus's blessing on same-sex love had to wait so long. There is no direct answer given, but it is clear that Simon's reaction to the love between Andrew and Philip was swift and violent, as it was rooted in the Jewish Law of the time, which would have demanded both be stoned to death. Perhaps Jesus had to weigh in the balance all he wanted to teach, along with the consequences each would bring. It is important, though, to credit Jesus with the selection of **four gay apostles out of twelve**: Andrew, Philip, Nathaniel (also called Bartholomew), and Labbaeus (also called Jude). This number was meant, perhaps, to compensate for the delay in the release of this key teaching, knowing they would spread the "discreet teachings" when so inspired by the Holy Spirit.

Perhaps the most proper way to close this last chapter, without turning it into another book, is to quote Jesus's comment about his disciples, found in Chapter 10:

"Do not suppose that I have chosen you twelve because

you are the holiest among all living men. Rather, you stand for *all men in all stages of spiritual understanding*, from John, the most enlightened, to Judas Iscariot, the most misguided. Except for him who shall betray me, future generations will call you all 'blessed' or 'Saint.' This is one of the paradoxes of this world, for nothing could be further from the truth. You, Andrew, and you, Philip, are among the closest to my heart. You alone followed the teachings of my messenger, John the Baptist, and you were the first to know me as a true son of God."

## Jesus, the Great Attainable Example

It is thus instructive to see Simon's dedication to the letter of the Jewish Law, while he misses its spirit. If you study the spirituality of Andrew, you will see his willingness to question seeming contradictions in the traditional understanding of Judaism, while being open to the presence of the Spirit in the beauty of nature, though Jesus encourages him to delve much deeper within, to discover the real reason for loving God. Philip seems to have a ready grasp of the deepest issues, which Andrew still struggles with, when faced with the entanglements of physical relationship. And John soars into the rarified air that Jesus has been breathing so remarkably, as he comforts Mary, the mother of Jesus, in the midst of the crucifixion, with sublime love and tenderness, and encounters, in his unified spiritual consciousness, Andrew and Philip on the missionary road. And, of course, Jesus himself represents *not* the *unattainable* ultimate to be worshiped, but rather the great and perfectly *attainable example* of awakened spirituality, as God has created him, as our elder brother who loves each of us with an encouraging and patient unconditional love, no matter our individual stage of spiritual understanding.

Let us, then, take the time to read and study and *live* this remarkable, miraculous document—announced by an angel—that it may serve its intended purpose. It has been received and released at this time to awaken us to our inner spiritual reality, that we might be a source of light and love and healing to our brothers and sisters. It has come to us now that we might serve to hasten the day when all division and strife and misunderstanding might cease, in the recognition that we are all the children of God, beloved by God, and in truth, one with All.

Atlanta, Georgia
November, 2013

# THE HEART OF JESUS'S TEACHINGS IN *THE BOOK OF ANDREW*

1.  **All love is holy** in the eyes of God, Andrew, whether it be the love of a man for a woman, a mother for her child, a man for another man, or a woman for another woman. You are as God created you. (p.30)

2.  I tell you this day, Andrew, that **you must be born again**. You will live many lives, until you have learned all the lessons you must master. You will live both as man and woman. In some lives you will love only women; in other lives, only men; and in still others, both women and men. This is true for all mortals.... (p.31)

3.  In truth, those we call mortals are immortal, from everlasting to everlasting. The body in which you dwell today is but the merest shadow of your eternal soul. Seeing that in different lives the same soul may love a man or a woman, **what can it matter** in the eyes of God whether you love a man or woman in this life, if only you love in God's name? (p.31)

4.  I bring you glad tidings of a new covenant. This is a true saying, yet it is false. No one except yourself can bring you news of the covenant. **You already hold in your heart** all that it says. You knew it to the letter when you dwelled in the Lord's own house. I only call it to your thoughts once

more. The unreal babble of the world so fills your ears and mind that you cannot hear the voice of God within your heart. (p.35)

5. **Whence comes the voice of God?** Neither from rocks of the mountain top nor from a burning bush nor from the thunder. Its dwelling place is in the soul of man. Was not Moses a man, very like yourself? Am I not a man also, created by God and born of woman, even as you? The Law of God has not been given to one man or one nation but to each man and woman and to all nations. You are chosen. (p.35)

6. For now I tell you only this: **think on the one word 'love,'** not earthly love that sets you apart and enslaves you, but love that makes us one in perfect freedom, the love of God, in all, of all, for all. I shall teach you so to love and so to live your life that men will mock you and persecute you. And the greater your love, the greater will be the rage of those with little understanding, seeing that you in turn will neither curse your persecutors nor disown your God. They will suppose you bolder than the lion, though what you have, in truth, is love not courage. Where there is naught to fear, who should have need of courage? (pp.36)

7. I tell you (Andrew) that **your love for Philip and Philip's for you is holy**, so long as you love in God's name. (p.46)

8. As we approached him, he turned to us and said, "I have been waiting for you and know what you seek. If you were born of the Spirit, you would not ask this thing of me. Yet you are men, and it is meet that **you should show**

**your love for one another with your bodies as well as with your hearts and minds.** Therefore, love one another joyfully, knowing that your mutual love for the God Who created us all will forge stronger ties between you two than any bond of flesh.

"As God has given you to one another, you have no need of any man's blessing, yet I will bless you. Give me your hands." Then he placed my left hand in Philip's right and clasped both his own hands about ours.

"You, Andrew, and you, Philip, shall love and cherish one another so long as you live, and even in death you shall never be parted." (p.47-48)

9. (Simon,)...this is why your spirit is troubled. It is because of **your concern for the opinions of men**. But should you not be even more concerned for the opinions of God? Like you I am an outcast to my neighbors and kinsmen. I am not welcome in Nazareth, for I have abandoned the trade of my earthly father and I have never taken a wife. Still, I do our Heavenly Father's will that I may be welcome in His house. (p.54)

10. Then Jesus said, "You are too much deceived by the appearances of the world created by men, where truth is not to be found. Can you not see that those who think themselves the rulers of the Earth are even more enslaved than those they subjugate? It is a far worse thing to work injustice than to suffer it.

"**I come to free men's Spirits, not their bodies,** by showing them the truth of God. He who has a free Spirit can never be enslaved, though he be shackled and cast into the darkest prison. On the other hand, he who has never learned the truth of God cannot be free in Spirit, even if all the world should call him 'Emperor'...only that man who has learned the truth of God is free in Spirit, and he who knows the truth of God can never slay anyone, under any conditions. Rather, he conquers his enemies with love, making them one with himself." (p.55)

11. "There are many," Jesus said, "who call themselves worshipers of the one true God but do not know that **in truth they worship false idols**. For the names of these gods are neither Baal nor Astarte, but vanity, ambition, worldly goods and power." (p.58)

12. Why do I say to you that it is easier for a rope to pass through the eye of a needle than **for a rich man to enter into the Kingdom of Heaven**? This is because the riches of the Kingdom—the fruits of the earth, the fish of the sea and the fowls of the air—belong to no one and to everyone. These are meant for all God's children.

There are enough of these riches for all, yet this is not the way of the world. Through their own trickery or the greed of their ancestors, a few have much more than they need while their brothers go naked and starve. Seeing that this is so, how can these few keep God's commandment to love their neighbors as themselves? I tell you that it is far better to go naked but to have a soul that is clothed in righteousness. ...in their hearts (the rich) know that they do not own the one possession worth the having. Their souls are like worm-eaten wood, for they have broken the highest Law of all.

In spite of this, I say to you that you should love the rich, who are your brothers and sisters. Though they would blind themselves, help them to open their eyes. Show them that the worldly goods they call most precious are like so many millstones hung about the soul unless their riches are shared with those who have nothing. (pp.58-59)

13. The Kingdom of God is everywhere at all times. The very ground we stand on now is part and parcel of God's Kingdom, as are the deserts, mountains, lakes and seas. **You will enter the Kingdom of Heaven as soon as you open your eyes**, seeking not to turn the things which are God's to your own profit but sharing these with all your brothers and sisters. (p.60)

14. In truth, **a man's senses are not five but twice five**. As a man's visible body has an invisible soul, so does each of the worldly senses have its counterpart in Spirit.

There are those who see, yet they are blind, as there are those who hear, yet they are deaf. By heeding too much the judgments of this world, they have robbed themselves of that second sight and second hearing which are God's gifts to everyone, even to those who are blind or deaf in the understanding of this world. ...if you put the teachings of the world behind you, always seeing with the eyes of Spirit, you will understand that even the serpent and scorpion are beautiful, as are those unfortunate men and women whom the worldly cast from their sight, calling them loathsome.

If you listen in the way of the world, you may hear a man cry out to you, 'Liar!' or 'Fool!' But if you **listen with the Spirit**, you will know this as the cry of one who dwells in darkness: 'Help me! I cannot hear God's voice nor see His face, wherefore I fear.' ...God speaks to men and women even today, giving aid and comfort to His children who love Him. Yet only those who listen with the ear of the Spirit shall hear His voice. (p.60)

15. Let us proclaim the one God, the God of His chosen people the Jews, Who is also the God of His chosen people the Egyptians, Greeks, Phoenicians and Romans. ...If you suppose that there are many tribes, it is only because you see others with worldly eyes and hear them with worldly ears. You make much of differences in their speech, the color of their skins, or the set of their cheekbones, but the many tribes you see are creatures of illusion, phantoms of your mind.

    In truth, **as there is only one God, so there is only one tribe**. As we are all sons of Adam and daughters of Eve, we are all brothers and sisters. Who, then, is your enemy?

    And if we are all of one tribe, so we have but one God, though men call Him by different names and worship Him in diverse ways, according to their understanding. Let all the people of the Earth raise songs of thanksgiving to the one God Who dwells in all our hearts. (pp.61-62)

16. If we grant that we own nothing, save our love for God and our neighbor, then we have all. **Love is the one eternal treasure**, the treasure no enemy can seize, the fortress that

is proof against all attack, the one jewel beyond price that no man may take from us, for we give it freely to all. (p.62)

17. ...**sin lies** not so much in those things which we do, as in what we fail to do. Remember that I have given you two commandments which stand above all others: That you should **love God** with all your heart and with all your soul and with all your mind, and that you should **love your neighbor** as yourself. Anyone who keeps these two commandments cannot sin. ...If your father and mother should say to you, "Slay your enemies! Wreak vengeance on those who do evil to you, taking an eye for an eye and a tooth for a tooth," then I say, "Dishonor your father and mother, for you have no enemies, only brothers and sisters." (p.63)

18. Surely you understand that you are to love God with all your heart and with all your soul. Many will suppose that is enough. Yet I have also told you that you should **love God with all your mind**. What do I mean by that?

   The purpose of the mind is always to **search for the truth beyond appearances**, with each using his mind according to the gifts that God has given him. ...Ever there is truth beyond truth, for you cannot know the whole truth so long as you are trapped in the illusions of this world. ...Some hold that, because an ancient prophet has inscribed words on a scroll, those words must need be true. Yet I tell you that **even those writings called sacred, being set down by men, mix truth with error**. Do not learn these words by rote, but **turn them over in your mind**, according

177

to the understanding God has given you, **asking yourself whether these writings are truly of the Spirit**, or whether they serve the worldly ends of those who seek dominion over others. ...Heart and soul and mind must each receive its just and equal due. (p.64-65)

19. I have given you the only prayer you shall ever need, but you are also free to create your own prayers, and to make of your life a prayer without words, by serving God with your whole being. You may begin by praying thus:

    "Our Father in Heaven, I love You, I praise You, I give thanks to You for the blessing of eternal life. Show me that sin is illusion, that only Your joy is real, seeing that I am forgiven as I forgive. Lead me not into temptation but deliver me from my own hardness of heart.

    "Let all my brothers and sisters share the daily bread which You have given. Help me to love all of Your other children as I love myself, that together we may enter Your Kingdom, for this is Your will. Amen."

    **You have no need to pray for other worldly things.** (p.65)

20. "If you see that the child's doings are indeed evil, what should you do?"

    "I should point out his error and show him the right thing to do."

    "That in itself would be an error," said Jesus, "for all you should do is love him all the more. **The child who knows perfect love can do no wrong.** It is only the want of love that leads children into error."

Then Labbaeus scratched his head and asked, "But if a child does wrong and goes on to do more wrong, who will correct the error?"

"God will correct it in time," Jesus answered, "through the love we show which comes from God. **Our love is all that can open the ears of others to the voice of the Holy Spirit within their own bosoms.**

"**This is the hardest lesson of love**. ...When I say to you that sin is illusion, I do not mean your own sins only." (pp.66-67)

21. "You say that **you love God, Andrew. Why do you love Him?** Is it because the Scriptures tell us that we must?"

"I have always tried to obey the Law," I answered, "but I love God still more because He has given us the world.... Wherever we turn, God's world delights our eyes.... Moreover, God has given us a never-ending feast for all our other senses as well..." Then Jesus said, "You speak of a world which you yourself have created. ...your eyes have never pierced the veil of illusion. You are blind to the true nature of God's creation. ...you must find another reason. ...If I should tell you, my answer would be mere words to you. The true answer to the question you have asked lies beyond words and even beyond the earthly senses."... "Where am I to find it?"

"Search your own heart and call upon the Lord." (pp.67-68)

22. If I am unlike other men, it is not that God has chosen me, but that I have chosen God. **Having learned all the lessons**

**of Heaven, I choose to do our Father's will rather than my own.** In this way I have gained perfect freedom over the madness and death of the world of men.

Men say that I work miracles. These miracles are but the power of God made visible through me. He is the Master, I am but the tool.

Through love and the power of God I have given sight to those whom the world calls blind. This is as nothing. It is a much harder thing to heal the blindness of those who see and believe the illusions of the world of men but not the truth of the Spirit, for understanding comes only from within. The eyes of the Spirit are opened only when you have said, "Henceforth I do the will of God rather than my own." (p.69)

23. In truth, I am the son of God, as you will also be when you have claimed your birthright. **If I am unlike you, it is only insofar as one blade of wheat stands higher than another, or as one lamp burns steadfastly while another flickers.** You are Andrew's elder brother of the flesh. I am your elder brother of the Spirit. (p.69)

24. When I say to all of you that your souls are eternal, I speak not only of Paradise and the life hereafter, but also of **other lives which are long forgotten**. Before Simon was, Simon was. Before Andrew was, Andrew was. Yet these brothers in blood shall be enslaved to the world until they become brothers in Spirit, to one another and to every other child of God, by attending closely to the lessons of Heaven and by freely choosing to do the will of Him Who is the Father of us all. (p.69-70)

25. I call on each of you today to choose joy over misery, freedom over slavery, life over death, and to **become the son of God you truly are**. (p.70)

26. ...why do we call God our Heavenly Father? Why should we not say, our Heavenly Mother? ...Man cannot create God. Nevertheless, our forefathers shaped a false vision of God arising from earthly pride, for they would see themselves as gods of this world, with dominion over the fowls of the air, the beasts of the field, and the fish of the sea. ...Men are the gods of the Earth only through cunning and brute strength. The living God, the Father and Mother of us all, rules not through force but with all-embracing love. ...**God, the eternal Spirit that gives us breath and being, is both man and woman and neither man nor woman.** If we are to feel within ourselves even the smallest part of God's glory, we must go beyond all earthly ideas and even beyond words. (p.70-71)

27. ...the **Law of God is written** not only on tablets of stone and in the Torah, but **in your own hearts** as well, and that which is written in your hearts **has greater authority** than cold words or dusty covenants. Therefore, be not troubled if the Law which the Holy Spirit has graven within your bosom contradicts the Torah, so long as you follow my commandment to love both God and your fellow man.

    It may be that your separate Law, given you by God, is not within the understanding of other men. Therefore, do not trouble their minds or burden their spirits with this seeming paradox, but rest assured that you are in truth a child of God and freely live by your own Law. ...it is good to follow the Scriptures, but if you study them too closely, you may find in them what is, in truth, not there. ...spend more time in listening to the voice of the Holy Spirit within your bosom and looking upon the message written on your own heart, and less in the study of books and the words of learned men who strain at gnats but cannot see the glory of the heavens. (pp.71-72)

28. ... **he who would find salvation must first find joy.** You should seek this joy in the worship of God, in doing good for others, and in those simple things which God has given you for this earthly life. Do not seek joy in worldly goods, for these are as spoiled fruit or sour wine. But no man can fathom the mystery or splendor of the simple things which God has given. ...be like little children, free of worldly ambition, pride, sin, and the burden of judging others, so that you may feel the endless joy of being a child of God. ...no suffering which men may inflict upon you can withstand the power of God's joy, whether they mock you or scourge you or strip you naked and nail you to a cross. (p.72-73)

29. I shall **unwind the meaning of parables** for you.... Remember first that in my parables I am always speaking of the Spirit and things of the Spirit. Remember also that things of the Spirit are to things of the world of men as day is to night, so that those things which appear to be contradictions may be reconciled, while those which appear to be the same thing may be very different. (p.73)

30. In the **parable of the talents**, the master of whom I speak is God Himself, and the servants are not two but legion, since they stand for all the peoples of this Earth. Yet through their actions they are but two kinds of men, the wise and unwise servants. ...At the time of each man's and each woman's birth, God bestows special gifts... Being gifts of the Spirit, these golden talents are not like worldly gifts, for they can be husbanded and increased only by lending them to others, for the glory of God's name and in the service of your fellow man. (p.73-74)

31. ...Jesus spoke further of his **story of the prodigal son**:

    "If a son should be away from his birthplace many years, would a father say, 'You may come home only if you take the straightest road?'...If God, our Heavenly Father, wants His children with Him, why should He not accomplish this at once, being all-powerful and knowing all? But God is loath to bring His children home in chains, like Roman captives. Rather He waits with loving patience till His children find their way to their Father, out of the fullness of their hearts and love for Him.

    "If a child be slow to learn, would a loving father kill him or cast him into darkness? No. Rather the father would cherish him all the more, repeating each lesson many times, till understanding dawns like a rising sun in mind and heart and soul." (pp.74-75)

32. **No one may master the lessons of Heaven in a single life**, but God, a loving Father, does not decree for His children the fire of eternal damnation. Rather, He repeats His lessons

with patience beyond the understanding of men, giving His children all the time they need to learn. This is why I say to you, you must be born again.

Time after time you will be born of the flesh, but when, after many lives, you have learned the lessons of Heaven, you will be born of the Spirit. From that time on, eternal Paradise is yours. (p.75)

33. ...Jesus also spoke to us of **healing**:

"Kings and tyrants may wreak suffering and death upon you, but this is as nothing against the suffering which you inflict upon yourselves, which men call sickness or possession by devils. ...I shall teach you how to heal the sick and cast out devils, but in truth these cures come to pass only through the will of God, when sufferers yield themselves up to His will and His love. For indeed, it is the sufferers themselves who bring the illness to their bodies. ...We shall cause those who feel themselves outside the Law to look upon the face of God, for one who has seen the face of God cannot be sick in body or in mind. ...We shall touch lepers and others whom men call untouchable, summoning forth the power of God which is in every man and woman, and making them whole. We shall make sickness health, sorrow joy, and darkness light." (p.75-76)

34. Before two Sabbaths have passed **I shall be put to death**.... I do not will it, nor does God. Nevertheless, I shall not prevent it, for man can be saved only through his own actions and by his own increase in understanding. Though I shall be put to death, I will not die. On the third day **I shall**

**rise from the dead**, but I will not stay with you for long thereafter. I must return to our Father. (p.81)

35. "First, **Andrew, I charge you to remember everything** that has passed between us, for false doctrines will be spread in my name, and seeds of judgment, hate and death will be sown by those who call themselves my followers. Also, I have told you things which are not to be given to the world at this time. Yet, when the time is ripe, you will open your heart and bear witness, setting down my true sayings that proclaim God's love for all His children."

    "How can that be, Lord," I asked, "seeing that I cannot write?"

    "I do not speak of this life, but of another long hence, when you will once again be a lover of men." (pp.82)

36. The second thing I would speak of is this: Remember that while God's Law is eternal and unchanging, man sees the Law only dimly, from afar, through the mists of this world of illusion. ...For this is the rule: the greater man's understanding, the simpler the Law. "That is why I have come into the world at this time. Before I came, there were ten commandments and many proscriptions. **I have given you two commandments** which replace all these: That you should love the Lord thy God with all your heart and with all your soul and with all your mind, and that you should love your neighbor as yourself. If only you keep these two commandments, you cannot sin. (p.82-83)

37. "Do not suppose that I have chosen you twelve because you are the holiest among all living men. Rather, **you stand for**

**all men in all stages of spiritual understanding**, from John, the most enlightened, to Judas Iscariot, the most misguided." ...Then I asked, "Where stands my brother Simon, Lord?"

Jesus frowned, and my heart sank when he answered: **"It is mainly through your brother Simon and another (Paul) who is not among the twelve that my teachings will be perverted and false doctrine spread throughout the world.** Future generations will make more of my death than of my life, more of my sorrows than of my joy.

"Simon will not reap the harvest, but he will sow the seed, not knowing where those things he does with good intent will lead. And people yet unborn will take Simon's greatest weakness to be his greatest strength.

"When I shall have left you a second time, Simon will take for himself the office of head priest, for he is not content to be only a fisher of men but would be a prince of this world. As I have said that the last shall be first, so must it follow that the first shall be last.

"In spite of this, you must still love your brother Simon, as I do. What he does, he does only through lack of understanding and not from want of love for me." (pp.83-84)

38. There are those who will becloud the minds of their brothers and sisters with incense, graven images and empty words that fall like tinkling brass upon the ear. **I am a man, even as you, but they will say that I am very God and that I came into this world as a sacrificial lamb.** Indeed, God is within me, and I am truly the son of God, as you are also,

yet the Lord our God Who created us all stands alone in majesty. There is none beside Him. (p.84)

39. **The one true church which is eternal lives**, but do not look for it in houses raised by men who serve the ends of future Caesars in my name. As I have said the whole world and all the heavens are God's church, can you suppose that man can shut it in with walls? (p.85)

40. Of all the followers of Jesus, **Judas was the only one whom Jesus had not called to himself**. When Judas came to the encampment at Cana to ask whether he might join the other disciples, Jesus said only, "Yes. I have been awaiting you." (p.88)

41. When next we were able to speak to Jesus alone, I said, "Master, I fear that Judas Iscariot is no child of God but a spy working for the high priest or the Romans."

"You are both correct and mistaken. Judas is an agent of the high priest. Indeed, when the time comes he will deliver me into the hands of the Romans, that I might be put to death. Yet Judas is also a child of God."

"This cannot be," I cried, "that a child of God should betray the very son of God! If he does this ungodly thing, I shall avenge you!"

"No vengeance will be taken, but the wrong will be righted."

"Who will right it?" I asked.

"Judas himself, though this will take many lifetimes. Whatever Judas does, you must not hate him, lest one error become two, for this is the way of the world. Remember what I have told you: that no one may harm the son of God, whose soul is beyond harm. **I command you to love Judas, for no man has more need of love.**" (p.89-90)

42. Suddenly a light appeared before us.... As the light faded, Jesus stood before us. "...it must be that what you come to tell us is a thing of great importance."..."I have come to remind you that there is much to do and little time. Along the path you have been following, shortly beyond this place, is a fork in the road. When you reach it, Philip shall take the path to the right, and you, the path to the left."

    "No!" I cried. "How can you ask this thing of us?"... "Though I have told you that your love for Philip, and Philip's love for you, is holy, **you must not lose your souls in the love of the body**. For many men and women, the love of the body is the highest rapture that they know on earth. Yet the love of the body is but the merest shadow of the true love of the Spirit, one thousandth of a thousandth part, as the light of a single lamp is to the sun. You yourself have caught some glimmer of that truth on this, your first mission.... The choice is yours alone to make, Andrew, but Philip counsels you wisely. Though the final lesson is always the hardest, do not protest. This is the lesson for which you have lived this life." (pp.107-109)

43. And though I died in pain and humiliation, stripped naked and nailed to a cross head down, I died in joy. For **my holy Master and Philip were there beside me** all the while, and in my heart, saying, "Beloved Andrew, you shall be with us in Paradise today!" (p.93)

44. "What wonders of creation children are! Lacking the heavy words that weigh down the spirit, the tearful memories of yesterday or the fears of tomorrow, they live in the eternal Kingdom of God—until we have taught them not to do so.

    "If you too would know the Kingdom of God, my dear followers and friends, **become like this child**. Forget all else, that you might recall the infinite goodness of Him Who is the Father of us all." (p.117)

45. "...there shall come a time long hence when all hearts shall be opened and everything which is in the soul of man made known. Then it shall be one thousand fold clearer than the light of midday that there is but one Law, and that this Law is eternal and unchanging. In that time of glory all men and all women shall be brothers and sisters, and all hearts and minds joined, for there will be no false or separate understandings of the Law....At the end of time and beyond time, the love of God in all, by all, for all will still all argument and right all error. Then all men and women will be brothers and sisters, for they will have found their way home." (p.71, p.85)

# SUGGESTED FURTHER READING AND WEBSITE SURFING

1.  *A Course in Miracles*, **Foundation for Inner Peace, P.O. Box 598, Mill Valley, CA, 1976. Website: www.acim.org.** If *The Book of Andrew* is Chuck Lehman's contribution to the ages, then *A Course in Miracles* is Bill Thetford's. Chuck's dear friend and former lover, Bill himself had discovered a previous life as the great early Christian theologian, Origen of Alexandria, c.185-254 C.E. Bill worked closely for many years with Helen Schucman, who received the thoughts of Jesus in a process that answered Bill's deepest yearning for "a better way."

    The result, *A Course in Miracles*, is a *massive* gift to the ages—a life-changing, spirit-awakening self-study program designed to clear the fog of the ego. With the help of the Holy Spirit, one's Inner Teacher, the student of this material will begin to understand and experience the reality of Spirit. When the controversy over being gay or lesbian finally settles down and becomes a non-issue, history will look back on these two gay men, Chuck and Bill, as giants in the spiritual field, for their contributions to the anchoring of spiritual truth to this earthly dimension.

2. **Dr. Kenneth Wapnick's Foundation for A Course in Miracles, Temecula, CA. Website: www.facim.org.** It is important to recognize the crucial role of Dr. Kenneth Wapnick in Chuck Lehman's awakening to his mission— to remember his life as Andrew. It was Ken's compelling inner vision and understanding that prompted him to share his insight with Bill Thetford: that Chuck was linked to the name Andrew. Chuck *knew* that he was supposed to do *something*, but without Ken's prodding, the book you are holding might not exist. Ken, in his own right, is a legend among *Course in Miracles* students, known for his exceptional intellect and generous heart in teaching and enlightening the *Course's* wisdom in workshops around the world, in books, DVDs, and CDs. Ken is dedicated to sharing a very clear, concise, and unadulterated vision of what Jesus has given us in *A Course in Miracles*.

3. **The Works of Dr. Brian Weiss**: For so many people around the world in the late 20th and early 21st centuries, the books, lectures, workshops, and CDs of Dr. Brian Weiss, eminent psychiatrist and beloved spiritual teacher, have been the most powerful voice for the reawakening of interest and practical understanding of reincarnation. Since the 1980s, he and his wife, Carol, have been tireless facilitators and advocates for those challenged by issues both physical and emotional that appear to be derived from past-life traumas. Many people will offer the exact same statement: "Dr. Weiss's books changed my life!" They certainly changed Dr. Weiss's life. He started as a classically trained psychiatrist from Yale

with a specialty in hypnosis, and no knowledge or interest in reincarnation or past-life regression.

As you will read in his first book, *Many Lives, Many Masters*, it was one of his patients' spontaneous memory of past lives—under hypnotic instruction to "go back to the source of the problem"—that literally stunned the good doctor into a broader and genuinely new awareness.

Each of his six main books is indispensable when it comes to understanding the many facets of reincarnation: *Many Lives, Many Masters: The True Story of a Prominent Psychiatrist, His Young Patient, and the Past-Life Therapy That Changed Both Their Lives; Through Time Into Healing; Only Love Is Real; Messages from the Masters; Same Soul, Many Bodies;* and *Miracles Happen.*

Website: www.brianweiss.com (Make sure to check out the excellent Reading List on his website.)

4. *Soul Survivor: The Reincarnation of a World War II Fighter Pilot* by Bruce and Andrea Leininger, with Ken Gross, 2009: A riveting account by the parents of a young boy who suffered from recurrent nightmares, including scenes of being trapped in a WW II fighter plane, on fire and about to crash. As his parents sought to comfort their child, they could not help but notice that he seemed to improve after sharing the details of his nightmare. His mother wondered about reincarnation as a way to understand her son's dilemma, while his father sought to research the details revealed in the nightmares to prove them *inaccurate*, fearing that proof of reincarnation might undermine his more

traditional Christian faith. The narrative reveals more and more pieces of the puzzle, both sourced from their son and from veterans' groups who remembered the fine young pilot who lost his life in the very crash their son had described. *Soul Survivor* is a gripping, moving account of a young boy who found healing and even renewed long-lost friendships, while his mother and father found a new depth of faith and richer meaning in their lives. Outstanding.

5. **The Works of Joan Grant and Denys Kelsey, MD**: No list would be complete without Joan Grant's seven ground-breaking "far memory" novels (*Winged Pharaoh, Life as Carola, Lord of the Horizon, Scarlet Feather, Eyes of Horus, So Moses Was Born*, and *Return to Elysium*). They were actually based on the past-life memories she derived from the deep reveries described in her book, *Far Memory*. She also wrote *Many Lifetimes* with her psychiatrist husband, Denys Kelsey, describing the remarkable healings and breakthroughs that came from combining her clairvoyant diagnostic talents with his gifts of hypnosis and psychiatry. A recent book, *Speaking from the Heart*, gathers the many wonderful unpublished writings that Joan Grant left behind, while Denys Kelsey's *Now and Then: Reincarnation, Psychiatry, and Daily Life* completes his views.

6. **The Works of Dr. Elaine Pagels, Princeton University.** In 1979, Dr. Pagels opened the door to the treasure trove of Gnostic wisdom found in the scrolls of Nag Hammadi, in *The Gnostic Gospels* and later in *Beyond Belief*. She revealed the missing pieces, also found in *The Book of Andrew*, that

the New Testament chose to avoid: that "self-knowledge is knowledge of God, and the self and the divine are identical; …instead of coming to save us from sin, (Jesus) comes as a guide who opens access to spiritual understanding; (and) when the disciple attains enlightenment, Jesus (and the disciple)…have become equal." See also Dr. Ken Wapnick's *Love Does Not Condemn*.

7. ***Never Forget to Laugh*, Carol Howe, 2010. Website: www. carolhowe.com.** Carol was a dear friend and confidant of Bill Thetford and provides a wonderful introduction to his life and his remarkable contributions to the world through ACIM.

8. ***The Unvarnished New Testament*, Andy Gaus, 1991.** This gifted translator has provided a vigorous, original, first-century version of the New Testament, without distortions, theological influences, and conjectures added centuries later. It used to be said that the four Gospels and the Acts of the Apostles were the best one could hope for in describing the life and teachings of Jesus, in spite of their distance in time from the original events. Andy Gaus's fresh, nonpartisan translation is a big help, but now, thank goodness, *The Book of Andrew* has, in my opinion, come to the rescue, revealing what Jesus really said and did.

9. **The Work of Professor Bart Ehrman, University of North Carolina, Chapel Hill.** Dr. Ehrman is the James A. Gray Distinguished Professor of Religious Studies and the best-selling author of a wide array of books reflecting a closer analysis of the New Testament. Starting off as a born-again

Christian and a devout student at the Moody Bible Institute of Chicago, the author continued his education at Princeton, only to discover that what he had earlier been taught about the infallibility of the Bible were not just mild overstatements, but actually dangerous falsehoods. That realization eventually led him to his present position of agnosticism about the truth of New Testament teachings, as they are so conflicted and often corrupted that he finds it hard to honestly know what Jesus really said or meant.

Here are some of Dr. Ehrman's books to consider: *Jesus, Interrupted: Revealing the Hidden Contradictions in the Bible (And Why We Don't Know About Them)*, 2010; *Misquoting Jesus: The Story Behind Who Changed The Bible and Why (Plus)*, 2007; *Forged: Writing in the Name of God – Why the Bible's Authors Are Not Who We Think They Are*, 2011. Website: www.bartdehrman.com.

10. **The Works of Dr. Jerry Jampolsky**. A gifted child psychiatrist and one of the earliest students and teachers of *A Course in Miracles*, Jerry founded the Centers for Attitudinal Healing, which have now spread worldwide (www.ahinternational. org). Jerry's many best-selling books, found on Amazon.com or at miraclecenter.org, have paved the way for a broad acceptance of the loving and forgiving attitudes contained in *Course* teachings.

11. **The Works of Marianne Williamson**: One of the most popular authors today in the field of spiritual awakening, Marianne Williamson found her voice, both inner and outer, in the study and teaching of *A Course in Miracles*.

Starting with *A Return to Love*, she has enriched our many conversations about the deeper life of the spirit. Website: www.marianne.com.

12. **The Past-Life Research of Dr. Raymond Moody**: Less well-known than his near-death-experience work is Dr. Moody's re-markable past-life research, found in *Coming Back: A Psychiatrist Explores Past-Life Journeys*, 1995, and *Paranormal: My Life in Pursuit of the Afterlife*, 2012. Outstanding.

13. **The Works of Gary Renard**: Gary's *The Disappearance of the Universe* sparked a renewed interest in *A Course in Miracles* among the *Course's* early students from the 1970s and 1980s , and touched many who had been unaware of the rich treasures of ACIM. He has continued the challenge with *Your Immortal Reality*, and his upcoming *Love Has Forgotten No One*. Website: www.garyrenard.com.

14. *The Search for Bridey Murphy.* How many books stay in print for fifty-seven years? First published in 1956, this classic tale of an Irish woman who spoke through a hypnotized patient is still fresh for today's New Age audiences, documented and proven through research and thorough experimentation. Morey Bernstein conducted a ground-breaking investigation of three post-war 1950s taboos: hypnotism, paranormal phenomena, and reincarnation. The author, a prominent, well-educated Colorado businessman and later philanthropist who started as a total skeptic and ardent materialist, encountered life-changing experiences about the human soul through each of the taboo areas. Bernstein is one of the

true founding pioneers of past-life regression, though he limited his trance efforts to finding solid data about the past life and times of the subject that could be later verified by independent researchers, rather than helping souls progress beyond past-life traumas toward wholeness. His findings are consistent, impressive, and important to what came later. His book is well written and compelling.

15. *Zealot* by Reza Aslan, 2013. This hugely welcome bestseller is perfectly timed to highlight the politically charismatic facet of the same Jesus who comes alive in *The Book of Andrew*—the Nazarene, not the Christ. The impassioned leader Aslan describes, coming from a town so humble it existed without a road, took as his first disciple Andrew, a man as illiterate as Jesus himself might well have been. Aslan's Jesus would also not have hesitated to accept and even sanctify a way of loving that was traditionally greeted with death by stoning, at the same time as he was leading a movement of the marginalized. Thankfully, to fill in the blanks left in Aslan's compelling secular portrait, we now have Andrew's own transcendent account of the zealously Spirit-led miracle worker we have longed to meet again.

Bruce Gregory
Editor

# ABOUT THE AUTHOR
# AND THE EDITOR
## OF *THE BOOK OF ANDREW*

C harles Cale Lehman (1926-1999), the author, was born in Camden, Arkansas and raised in Memphis, Tennessee and Tupelo, Mississippi. Valedictorian of his high school as well as his Millsaps College graduating class, he attended the Graduate Faculties at New York's Columbia University, 1955-1959, graduating with an M.A. in Social Psychology. He served in the United States Navy and was proud of his military service to his country, though he never saw enemy action. Charles also proudly served as an officer of an organization of gay veterans in New York until close to his death. A New Yorker, his main career was in marketing and advertising research, but his deepest loyalties concerned his friends and his Lord.

Charles Cale Lehman
during World War II

B ruce Gregory, the editor of *The Book of Andrew* and facilitator of Charles's regressions, was born in Savannah, Georgia in 1945 and raised in Atlanta. He majored in French at Davidson College and the Universite de Montpellier in France, and earned an MBA in marketing at The Wharton School. A minor health issue prevented his military service in Viet Nam, inspiring him to dedicate the two years he might have served to a search for deeper understanding of God, leading him to Spiritual Frontiers Fellowship and life-long spiritual friends who opened remarkable doors. After four years as a financial analyst and manager at the CBS Television Network in New York City, Bruce took a short sabbatical to visit Sathya Sai Baba in India before returning to a new career as an Instructor and Graduate Program leader at Silva Mind Control. After two successful years, he was fired for simply being gay. Alerted by a New Year's premonition that he would soon encounter revolutionary new life-changing material that would represent the height of practical spirituality, he was introduced to *A Course in Miracles* and to its scribes, Helen Schucman and Bill Thetford, in the very first week of 1976, six months before it was published. Bruce went on to become one of the first teachers of *A Course in Miracles* in New York City, while also working with past-life regression techniques and leading workshops in spiritual healing. In 1979, he left NewYork with friends to live in rural Arizona, working as a substance abuse counselor at the state prison in Safford for thirty years, creating innovative programs that were adopted statewide. He is presently retired and has relocated to Atlanta, Georgia.

Bruce Gregory (left) and *Course in Miracles* co-scribe Bill Thetford in Tiburon, California, 1979

The Round House Press, a small independent publisher, is proud and grateful to have developed *The Book of Andrew* over the last several years, publishing this lifesaving book without having to answer to corporate or other constraints and limitations.

Bruce Gregory and I, the original Team Andrew, welcome our fellow team members, and will gratefully accept contributions that would ensure *The Book of Andrew* the global reach it deserves. Such contributions, which will be acknowledged in future editions, should be sent to The Andrew Project, c/o The Round House Press, PO Box 744, Kent, Connecticut 06757. Checks should be made out to The Round House Press.

Continuing to publish independently and courageously throughout the world is the ideal way for this long-awaited Voice to be heard.

Patricia G. Horan
Editor and Publisher
The Round House Press

CPSIA information can be obtained at www.ICGtesting.com
Printed in the USA
BVOW02s1559270915

419774BV00002B/11/P